LEARNING
WITH THE CHALLENGING CHILD

Forty Years of Learning From
Educationally Handicapped Children

Grace Petitclerc

LEARNING WITH THE CHALLENGING CHILD

Forty Years of Learning
From Educationally Handicapped Children

LEARNING WITH THE CHALLENGING CHILD

Forty Years of Learning
From Educationally Handicapped Children

Grace Petitclerc

Academic Therapy Publications
San Rafael, California

Contents

Foreword

FORTY YEARS OF TEACHING educationally handicapped children is an impressive background for any dedicated teacher. For Grace Petitclerc, one who is certainly an exceptional person as well, it has created an opportunity to combine her very unique perceptiveness with realistic practical application.

We are fortunate that, through this volume, she has chosen to share the wealth of her success — drawn from her rich background and broad experience. The lucid descriptions of her accomplishments with individual cases document her depth of understanding, the extent of her conviction and the valid effectiveness of her wide and imaginative range of techniques.

Long before the development of today's (still incomplete) categorization of brain dysfunction (neurological handicap), she appreciated the interrelationship of some sort of complex "physical-emotional dysfunction" and the processes of learning — and of school success. As we become more sophisticated in diagnosis of these defects through knowledge gained from medical science and as we more diligently attempt to appreciate the inherent capacity of these children, we will understand more fully why her methods have met with so much success.

It is the task of others of us to effectively seek out and document the relationships of a multiplicity of health and emotional factors to many aspects of school success, and through this knowledge to look for ways to help all school children. Mrs. Petitclerc has demonstrated that, in the meanwhile, we need not always wait — insofar as the educationally handicapped child is concerned — until complete and absolutely accurate diagnosis is determined before offering some special educational assistance. She has dramatically described the effectiveness, within an appropriate educational setting, of accepting him, of attempting to understand him and of utilizing a wide variety of methods in helping him realize his individual inherent potential.

B. OTIS COBB, M.D.
Assistant Professor, Health Education
Stanford University
Director, California Joint Study of
Student Health Problems and School
Performance.

In her book, STAND TALL AND LOOK FAR, Grace Petitclerc has given the interested public the characteristics of Neurologically Handicapped Children which distinguish them from the Mentally Handicapped, with whom they have been confused. Further, she has demonstrated the quality and principles of teaching that these characteristics require.

While these principles underlie the guidance of all children, they are critical for the NH Child. The adult's help can be accepted and utilized by the child only when some special interest of his has been discovered mutually, through which he can actively contact his environment and learn from it. Once this is achieved, the child is freed for goal-directed effort and achievement and he educates himself rapidly and broadly.

Mutual affection and trust between adult and child build security so that the child can act freely. Mutual respect builds the child's respect for himself which promotes his goal-directed effort. On this foundation the NH Child can accept help from the adult that reinforces the child's effort so that he can succeed. The achievement of this vantage point is facilitated, in large part, by parental understanding and active cooperation in the child's development. The adult's approval labels his successful efforts so he builds his own set of values and approves of himself.

Ample evidence of the above statements is found in the case studies presented and the insightful commentaries by Mrs. Petitclerc. Successful results are highlighted by the cases in which the child tries to shift to classroom teaching in public or private schools. A few failed disastrously when the understanding of the teachers was inadequate. But others succeeded with academic learning and quickly added social learning. This is very reassuring and challenging.

Mrs. Petitclerc's unprecedented success in guiding NH Children presents a challenge to educators to develop a graduated program for these children which offers the necessary individualized situation and guidance from the beginning, then, as it can be accepted, companionship and small group experience, and finally classroom participation. We greatly need specialized teachers *now* to take over and carry on from gifted teachers, like Mrs. Petitclerc, who have discovered the NH Child and revealed his needs and his potentials, and shown us how to free him for self-directed learning. In time, all teachers may gain from learning how to meet the needs of NH Children

We beg of Mrs. Petitclerc that she share with us the wealth of her experience, by word of mouth or published material, that we may have many more case studies with insightful commentaries that draw our attention to the process involved in achieving success. Thus offering to those of us who are eager to learn about the NH Child excellent self-teaching material.

ETHEL B. WARING, Professor Emeritus
Cornell University, Ithaca, N.Y.
Dept. of Child Development and Family Relations

1. The Beauty of His Rare Potential

Ŋ EPTEMBER, 1920, in a one-room unpainted
frame school house near the Columbia River, Danny Hines sat in the third
row, last desk — two sizes too big for him — his shiny blue eyes fixed on
his new teacher. His eager questioning face attracted me immediately.
Such a beautiful boy . . . sturdy and rosy cheeked, with a shaggy mop
of curly black hair.

Calling the roll that first morning, I asked for his name and grade,
and a child in one of the front seats answered for him. At my quick
reprimand, the child explained gently, "But, Miss, you don't know about
Danny. He don't talk very good. He don't learn nothing, either. He just
sits here all day long. His pa thinks some learning might rub off on him.
Any how, that's what we guess."

That shook me. I had never seen anyone who could not learn, except
an idiot, once. This boy was no idiot. An intelligent mind looked at me
out of those astounding eyes.

The records showed that Danny had been in school for three years
and that no learning had resulted. A hurried telephone call to the County
Superintendent for help and advice brought another shock. "Let that boy
alone!" the gentleman on the other end of the line shouted. "His dad is
clerk of the Board and I've had enough trouble with him about that kid.
If you stay out of it, I can recommend that the youngster be sent to the
state institution at the end of this year. Now, just quiet down, let the boy
alone, and go on with your teaching."

Angry and outraged, I turned to the parents. Danny's father, a wealthy
orchardist, shouted in my face, too. He waved his arms and beat his fists
on the table deprecating schools and everyone connected with them. Danny
had readily learned to run a new tractor, why was it such a job to get
him to add two and two or read a book? He had brains, that boy did.

The little mother wept as she followed me out of the house. She
explained that Mr. Hine's brother had been like Danny and the family
had been forced to put him away before he was twenty. "Joe, my husband,
nearly went out of his mind," she said. "Now, our doctor tells us we'll
have to do the same with Danny."

"Mrs. Hines," I said, "do you ever pray?" This was a final trump. I
must have someone *with* me.

"Oh, yes, most all the time."

"Then pray with me that Danny will learn this year."

After agreeing to this, she also consented to let Danny come to school an hour early each morning, presumably to help with various duties in the classroom. I was determined to have time with him when no prying eyes or active resistance could deter whatever we might find profitable to do. I meant to find a way, however extreme, to make him learn. That determination so dominated all my waking thoughts that at last an idea of where to start did come to mind.

Danny liked to play ball. However, he said *baw* for *ball,* and maybe, if he learned to spell the word, if he became familiar with the letters and how they went together in writing and saying the word, maybe he would have something from which to achieve more. There was no harm in trying it, anyway.

I held his hand and we wrote the word on the ball, saying the letters as we wrote. Then, each time we threw the ball we said the letters and the word. After two weeks, Danny still said *baw,* and could not spell the word when asked.

To the throwing and saying, we added puffing out the letters with a loud exaggerated breath, in and out. Next, we wrote the letters on the toes of his shoes to look at and say as he stamped around the school yard. He also wrote the word on the board with his fingers, my hand over his, at first, then by himself. He wrote with chalk on the board, with a pencil on paper and with a knife in dirt.

Then, one day, lo and behold! he could say the word *ball* in its entirety and spell it.

Country schools of that period often turned Friday afternoons into a Spelling Bee, each grade competing at its own level. However, when Danny was out of the room I asked the other students, fifteen in all, if they would allow him to step above anyone of them, even the Eighth Graders, every time he spelled his one word right. They liked Danny and wanted to help him, so they eagerly fell in with the plan.

That afternoon, step by step, he climbed to the head of the line. Suddenly looking around, he realized, all at once, where he was, what he had done, and he stood a moment, transfixed. Then, he leaped into the air and yelled, "By God! I'm the best speller in the whole school!" Every word perfect.

Streaking out the door and across the playground toward home, he never stopped yelling, "I'm the best speller in the whole school!"

From that day he began achieving.

A number of years later a friend in that district wrote me of Danny being married, of his success in running his own orchard and of his work with the Agricultural Agent on cross-pollination.

2. The Teacher as Learner

FACED with educating a neurologically impaired child certain basic principles always stand out for consideration. First, our own attitude.

Look at him. Is he a beautiful child, perfect in physical form, bright-eyed and eager? I have never met an NH Child who was not. Even without speech or muscular control, and with little ability to show evidence of any aptitude, this child is very different in appearance and action from the mentally retarded. Observing him, words from a famous play come alive: "There's nothing ill can dwell in such a temple!"

This conviction is adamant for us who educate. We must hold to it against all odds, or we are defeated before we begin. Where no expectation stands, nothing is revealed in any field of exploration.

We hold that there is a potential within this child sufficient and worthy to be liberated, that no effort is too great, no resistance too formidable to prevent our penetrating the barrier which hides his capacity. In forty years of teaching such children, I have never failed to find what I *expected* was there to find.

The undeniable results of some rather bold expectations have led me to believe that the NH Child is an entirely unique and highly promising individual whose depths have not yet been adequately plumbed. Having been recognized as having capacity only in the last few years, he is, even now, making a notable contribution to humanity's new frontier:

1. He has stimulated long-overdue research on brain structure and function, bringing facts to light which bend our attitude; for example, the brain is *not* the mind (it is merely the instrument of the mind), cells surrounding injured brain tissue can and will, with proper training, take over the function of lost areas.

2. Because, fortunately, he is unique even in the injury itself — no two injuries occur in exactly the same brain area with the same involvement — medical statement, psychological theory, educational philosophy and method are therefore occupied with a number of changing attitudes and practices. None of our former practices, tests or techniques are effective with the NH Child. Thus his dynamic need, like a cyclotron, is breaking up crystalized concepts and making way for fresh ideas which, ultimately, will benefit all children.

3. When this child's potentials are at last released and examined, there is no doubt — in my mind — they will be found to be of

exceptional nature, high in worth, rare in intense drive, and intuitive in character. The effect of stimulating hitherto dormant brain areas seems to be that previously concealed doors, open; so the NH Child will always appear a little different to us because he reaches into unusual levels of thought.

Therefore, it is actually we who are learning from him. He presents us with the most challenging adventure life can offer: exploring brain and mind and creating means to bring them into a functioning unit. It is a singular privilege to serve this intent.

Each day, we who educate the neurologically impaired are called upon to restate our radiant confidence and reaffirm our determination to triumph. This attitude pierces any obstacle, gives any pursuit a glow of excitement and marshals all our assets and forces to the job ahead.

3. Changing the Image of Self

THE SECOND basic principle to consider is the child's attitude. He also must be convinced of his capacity.

If you get him young, before frustration and failure have erected their barbed defences, this initial step is comparatively easy. However, each added year, past five, multiplies and compounds the difficulty. So get him young, even very young.

There are some children I have known who would have been lost entirely if they had been left without help at an early age. Melvin Tully was one of these. He was in deep trouble when he entered Kindergarten.

His first day at school he blacked two boys' eyes and cracked open another one's skull with a rock because they laughed at the tonal garble he used for speech. The second day he made a barricade of wooden blocks in one corner of the schoolroom from which he threw blocks at the rest of the class. When the teacher's back was turned, a boy ran up and kicked down one side of the barricade and Melvin proceeded to take the room apart, bit by bit. The class fled, genuinely frightened by his screams and grimaces. When in this mood he did, for a fact, take on the appearance of being possessed.

Melvin had other difficulties besides speech and lack of control. Memory played odd tricks on him. Things he wanted to forget, he was never able to get rid of; and those he tried to remember faded even as he was experiencing them. He stumbled over his own feet and dropped things he picked up, and always banged against the door frame as he went rushing out the door. Yet, I have never known a boy who wanted more to excel, who yearned more for admiration.

In 1956, when he was nine and we had worked together for three and a half years, his family moved to Switzerland. There, he and his two brothers learned to carry on their schoolwork in German, French and English. Now, at seventeen, Melvin is finishing the equivalent of our Highschool and serves as assistant ski instructor at the school, a responsible, well-composed young man.

Think of what might have been his end if he had gone on another year in the direction he was turned at five.

Nonetheless, at whatever age the child begins his association with you, the initial act between you — the cornerstone of his attitude — is an act of mutual cooperation. Cooperation forms the substructure of any relationship.

I have often been asked, "How do you get the cooperation of a child who pays no attention to your overtures, verbal or physical, and cannot stand still long enough to be caught by some interest?"

There are, of course, as many ways as there are children. Each teacher must find that particular key which will hold a particular child in a particular situation. There are no formulae. Each of these children is as distinct from the other as crystal patterns in snowflakes, each a unique creation that responds uniquely.

However, by observing a few responses of children who took the first step into cooperation, the substance of some ideas for your situation will germinate:

> Payton Collins, dark eyed and brittle as an active cricket, with no speech, nor any reaction to speech, completely disregarded every overture I made. He dashed around the room from one object to another, totally ignoring my presence; even attracted by a ball of dust in one corner but unaware of a monkey on a string over his head.

> After I had tried everything I could think of to hold his eye or ear, I suddenly picked up two long wooden blocks and slapped them together with a sharp whack. He ducked his head and clapped his hands over his ears. Evidently the noise hurt.

> I slapped the blocks again, then handed them to him, indicating with my hands over my ears that he could hurt me in the same way. He grabbed the blocks and slapped them together with a tremendous whack.

> I winced, then laughed, as if it were fun even though it hurt. A faint grin appeared at the corners of his mouth. We were playing and he liked it. "Do it again," I said, in word and gesture. He did, several times.

> *Then he handed the blocks to me,* smiled and nodded his consent to a turn at being hurt.

> Thus our cooperative companionship began.

Cooperation soon grows into an affection, a mutual respect, that melts resistances. With Alan Zucker this was a rewarding development.

> At five Alan produced a score on an IQ test that assured his family they had another genius — his father is a prize-winning physicist. Because of his sparkling personality and handsome mold, his lagging achievement in school the first year was hardly remarked

Andy's finger painting of stiff trees done in kindergarten style—response of child's first step into cooperation.

Andy's landscape in oils, done very professionally. Now he is able to prosper in a group, with a group, and contribute to a group.

upon. But when he turned seven and still had not learned to read or to write, everyone was shocked, dismayed and mystified. And Alan, a very large boy, seemed to shrink two sizes.

He began playing hookey from school or stayed home, pretending an illness to avoid the consequences of his discrepancies in the classroom. Then he started lying to parents and school authorities concerning his whereabouts when he was neither at home nor at school. And something had to be done.

Wrapped in stony resistance he stalked through some games with me at our first meeting, at which time I determined the points of need where we might begin work. He could not ride a two-wheel bike, carry a tune or distinguish colors; he was left-handed and left-footed, but right-eyed; he could draw large figures but could not follow the outline of small figures or symbols, even of the size found in preprimer books.

Our second meeting he willingly played a game of darts, though he cheated to win. And I said, "I wouldn't cheat you, because I'm your friend; and I know you are my friend, too. Friends don't do that kind of thing to each other." His lower lip hung for a moment, then he looked up and said sincerely, "I'm sorry. I won't do it again."

Then, at our fifth meeting, I felt we were ready, and I approached him head-on. "Alan," I said, "you are a very bright boy. I couldn't fool you in any way, or make you do something you didn't want to do; and you know I wouldn't want to do that. You are fully aware that you have come here so I can help you learn to read, perhaps to write. But I promise you I'll never ask you to read or do anything you don't think is fun until you tell me you are ready to work hard. Now, so I won't make a terrible mistake by planning something you don't want to do, tell me what you think is fun."

A torrent of pent-up words broke loose, like the lifting of a flood gate. It seemed that he had never been asked before what he would like to do and his towering desire to choose his own special high time reached back to preschool days. Holding up my hand to stop the verbal outpouring for a moment, I cried, "Wait! This is too interesting to lose! Let me take it down." And I sat at the typewriter.

He grinned, pleased and relaxed. Stretching his feet out on another chair, he sighed and said, "Gosh, this is the life. Ready, secretary?"

Cooperation must reach this place of loving trust. The tremendous effort you have to demand of a child with deepseated needs requires the utmost between you. Unlike the mentally retarded, the NH Child requires the support of your demand on his performance up to and a fraction beyond his level of fatigue, in the same manner that a physiotherapist stretches his patient's endurance a little farther each day past the point of comfort. There should also be rhythmically spaced periods where all demand is suspended, periods of rededication of teacher and child to greater effort and more exacting demands. For you are dedicated to never give up until the goal is overtaken, and this takes cooperation of the hardiest nature.

The essential of cooperation — co-operation — must also take effect deep within the child's own body:

Hands and eyes must learn to work together.
To this team the action of the feet is added.

Nerve and muscle throughout the body must be
taught to operate smoothly and jointly.
To this team the senses are added.

Brain and body must acquire an affinity that
not only bridges the injured areas but assists
willingly in the stimulation of new ones.
This team must become the skilled agents of the mind.

When cooperation is attained in this circuit you have a child, NH or otherwise distractible by nature, who can sit down, pin his attention on a task and begin to learn. Here, again, I have been questioned: "How do you help a child attain this alliance within himself?"

This pia mater in the process of learning requires more than a brief commentary on it. Let us give it full consideration in the next section. However, may I augment the importance of inner cooperation by saying here, that the child begins to learn because, at this point, he has begun to feel his own worth. Then, once having felt his ability to handle himself, he finds he is also able to prosper *in* a group, to prosper *with* a group, and contribute *to* a group.

It is an exciting moment to see this taking effect in a group of children:

Eight six year olds with serious problems had each been helped to accept his environment in a one-to-one conditioning, then brought into a group where he had to accept others in a different environment and conditioning. Some rough spots were still apparent in the group's relationships after a full week.

On this particular morning a pleasant sounding bell summoned the group into the talking circle for an important discussion. Obediently, each dropped what he was doing and carried his chair to the open space at the side of the room, all except Jory. He stood at the sink washing cups and tidying up after our ten o'clock snack.

Until that day Jory had refused to take any responsibility in the class or to share labor of any kind. Yet, there he was, humming softly to himself, absorbed in the work of cleaning up a rather large group mess. Whatever this total absorption may have meant to any other child, for him it was a major breakthru.

The children looked at me to see if I were going to remind him that we were waiting for his cooperation. When I said nothing, the one little girl in the group turned to the others and explained the situation.

"You see," she said, with elaborate nicety, "he is so happy to do some work for us, now that he's decided to be a good neighbor, we just have to let him be what he's decided to be."

Thereupon, everyone waited, cooperatively.

Another morning, in another group, Billy brought his little brother John, of whom he was very proud, to visit our class. Billy had no speech but that did not deter him from making little brother known to his classmates by head nods, smiles and gestures as little brother spoke his own name.

Each child accepted the introduction cordially. Then, the two brothers stood before Roy, a sullen discontent in the making, if there ever was one. He sat looking at a book and would not lift his eyes.

Billy touched Roy on the shoulder. No response. Next he pulled and pushed at the stubborn boy trying to get him out of his seat, but to no avail.

By this time the whole class was watching.

Billy then tried to pull Roy's head back and lift up his eyelids so he would have to look. But the mulish boy was not going to acknowledge little brother. He drew his head into the protection of his shoulders, shut his eyes and, turtle-like, remained impervious to coercion.

Richard, a boy who sat on the other side of Roy, suddenly jumped out of his seat, grabbed the book out of Roy's hands and bopped him over the head with it. "Say 'Hi', to Billy's brother!" Richard ordered.

Roy looked disdainfully at the little fellow, rubbed his aching head and mumbled off-hand, "Hi, Squirt."

Richard demanded sternly, "Say Hi, *John!*"

Roy looked around the class. The expression on every face echoed Richard's demand. And Roy cooperated.

In what terms do you suppose a child evaluates himself when he realizes all at once that he can do certain things he was never able to do before? As he begins to like the give and take between himself and his teacher, as he recognizes that the freedom he has within the firm structure of routine is good, that others like him and support his efforts, what happens to him inside?

No doubt he feels as if he has just awakened from a bad dream. Gradually, all the things he imagined about himself beforehand lose their reality, and his "self-image" begins to change.

4. The Art of Relaxation

THE FINAL MEASURE in bending the child's attitude, that it may serve to his benefit, is relaxation. Together, cooperation and relaxation form a solid foundation on which to build the process of learning.

Surface relaxation has already begun during the various levels of emotional release experienced with cooperation. It is needful, however, for the NH Child, in common with the great majority of us, to be able to relax consciously, physically, emotionally and mentally.

The art of relaxation must be learned step by step, and practiced diligently, day by day. Many classes have quiet periods where the children rest their heads on their desks, some even have children stretch out on blankets. But this is not enough. Here is the opportunity to relax, yet few, if any, know how and the opportunity is lost. Conscious relaxation requires a formula that replaces the habit pattern of tensions controlling the muscle-nerve-emotional-mental structure. And each layer in that multiple structure must be educated separately, then coordinated into a single working unit.

As with all procedures, there are as many ways of introducing relaxation to children as there are children, and each child, having his resistances and fears in a pattern peculiar to himself, answers an approach peculiar to that pattern. Unless we meet this peculiar position in which his tensions lie, he goes on holding his resistances against learning, and against relationships in general. Here again we experiment with every approach we can think of, until he is touched in the right spot.

A common approach is through the rag doll idea. The child is given a rag doll to feel, to flop around and then try to imitate the loose feel and the flopping arms and legs. It works with some children, but I had a little girl with whom I practiced four years before she could flop her arms and legs like a rag doll.

She was a delightful little redhead named Margie Carter, four years seven months when we met. Her beautiful brown eyes did not focus; the right eye rolled toward the nose when it was asked to function and remained there until the demand was released, and the left eye seemed to see only bits and pieces. She crawled up the four steps to my door and slid down when she left, and her pretty little hands could neither grasp nor hold an object of any size.

When we tried to relax, every muscle in her body bristled like hair on a dog's back. I experimented with all the known approaches and several dozen unknown ones, then, at last, I just picked her up bodily, laid her out on a couch and held her down until her muscles quieted. Next, I spread one arm and the upper part of my body over her and, with the other hand and arm, began moving her arms, one at a time, then her legs. Each time a part of her body was moved the whole of it recaptured its tension, but finally, after months of practice, she could have one part moved and the rest would stay quiet.

Then, still more months passed before she could move an arm herself and keep the rest of the body quiet. Next we moved the fine muscles, the fingers, toes and tongue in all directions while keeping the large muscles relaxed. Then, from crawling we learned to walk up and down stairs, from lying prone to feel relaxation we learned to sit and stand and retain the same feeling. And, after four years, besides being able to do most of the patterned expectations for an eight year old, she could also shake herself like a rag doll.

And her eyes were straight. And she could talk and read and write, and now goes to public school.

Should we ever give up?

The art of relaxation progresses from a surface release of rigidity to a complete liberation of the muscle-nerve structure from all conscious control. This latter is accomplished lying prone, in the initial stages of learning the skill. The formula then advances into conscious relaxation in which each section of the body is taught to release its fear imprints, as well as to *establish* mobility and control if that contact has not been made before.

It is at this point that cooperation takes effect deep within the child's own body:

1. Induce complete release through music, soothing sounds — on records, quiet-toned directions, massage, warm applications, or any means that will produce a profound stillness inside the body to the end that sleep is just one step away. This should be practiced a great number of times before going beyond it.

Now direct the child to roll his hands into very tight fists, so tight he can feel every muscle straining in them. Let them relax. Do this again and again, until the conscious relaxation in the hands becomes a skill the child can bring about at will, without tensing the muscles first.

Practice the same way with each finger, until the detail of every muscle, separately, in the hand has its own control center in the brain that can be operated at will.

Bring about the same control in the feet, muscle by muscle. Let the child press his feet against a flat surface — wall or box or such — so the feel of tension goes up the legs and the feel of release then affects the whole lower part of the leg. Bring the toes and the arch of the foot into this frame of control.

Move to the eyes. Squeeze the lids together, tight, tighter, tighter; then release them. Repeat this a number of times. Place a cold metal disc — a penny, dime, or such — on the closed eyelids and mentally follow the sensation of the cold disc on the lid as it descends through the eyeball and into the muscle-nerve cluster behind, releasing all tension in the wake of the coolness. Lying relaxed, put the palms of the hands over the closed lids and keep them there until a different sensation of relaxation results from the even warmth descending through the eyes. Repeat these exercises until the eyes will release their tensions at a mental command.

When these controls are established, performed with effortless ease, with the rest of the body relaxed and uninvolved, then put the coordination of hand and eye to work. Begin while still lying down so the rest of the body remains relaxed, setting a memory pattern for eye-hand coordination operating in other positions.

Make a circle on a large piece of paper and hold it at an easy distance directly above the child. Direct his eyes to follow around the rim of the circle to the left, then to the right. Add the forefinger of the right hand following around the circle with the eyes, then the forefinger of the left hand.

Make a line through the middle of the circle, first a vertical one, next a horizontal, then a diagonal. Have the eyes begin at the top point of contact between line and rim, go down the line, then around the rim, to left then right. Add the forefinger of the right hand to the eye movement, then the forefinger of the left hand. Change by beginning at the bottom point of contact between the line and the rim of the circle.

Make a dot in the middle of the bisecting line and begin the exercise from that point, first up and around the rim, then down the radius and around the rim.

Repeat these exercises with different forms: rectangles, triangles, figure eights. Now sit up and do the same across the room. Finally carry the eye-hand cooperation into throwing games, finger painting, writing.

Lastly, add the feet in the exercises lying down, in the same exercises with the geometric forms on the floor — feet following eyes, then in kicking games and bare-foot fun in wet clay or finger paints. Now take to walking a straight line — eyes and forefinger of dominate hand pointing on the line while the feet carry a body kept tonally relaxed; leaping from one circle marked on a walkway to another; jumping rope — the child turning his own rope — or balancing on a jumbo-ball.

Conscious relaxation finally brings a habit of ease, the relaxed approach to any action of mind or body. This skill is peremptory for the NH Child.

Bobby Rusk, when he was told we were going to explore something new, would always ask, "Is it going to be hard?"

"Yes, it is going to be hard, until you learn how, then it will be easy," I would reply. It is an important part of the therapy for these children that they always know where they stand and how far they have to go to reach success.

"Then, I guess I had better take my exercises." And he would go lie on the floor, do a few movements of tension and release, then in the stillness of his own quiet body prepare himself for the challenge.

Great athletes prepare themselves thus. They set their muscle structure in position for their specific athletic performance, then relax, completely at ease, pliant and resilient. The command for action must travel over yielding, cooperative nerve and muscle if accuracy and endurance of championship standard is to result.

Fortunately, for me, one of the first children brought to me for help taught me the intrinsic value of yielding, cooperative nerve and muscle, brain and body.

Ted Dunn was ten, but he looked as if he had stopped growing at six. He was red haired and brown eyed, and freckled, with belligerence sticking out of every fiber.

His mother dragged him into my house one day and asked bluntly, "Do you think you could teach this kid to draw?"

At that time I occasionally took art students. "We could try," I answered.

"Well, he can't seem to learn anything at school. He's ten and hasn't learned to read, yet. And he has to learn *something*. See what you can do."

I picked up a carnival hat lying on the table and playfully put it on Ted's head, hoping to make a favorable impression on the boy. The hat had a couple of feathers on the right side, stuck in at a horizontal slant, and five small bells on the left side with a pom-pom on the peak.

"Close your eyes," I said, "put up your right hand and feel what is on your head."

He raised his left hand and waved it back and forth in an attempt to touch his head. Finally he found the bells, but could not count them. I helped his right hand to hit the feathers, and he could not determine whether they stuck up or down or out. So we avoided the pom-pom.

I began to wonder how I was going to teach him to draw. Wonder turned to bewilderment when I gave him a pencil and paper and tried him out in making circles and lines. His hands were like robot's, striking out stiffly in any direction without control or purpose.

Whatever we did together, it would have to start at a point far back of the concept of representation. And where was that? I puzzled.

Drawing is very old in the history of man. What skills had early man perfected that he used to begin pictorial representation? He felt things, of course, with all parts of his body, and smelled them and, eventually, looked at them. Did he remember them in visual images? He would have to, to represent them in a picture.

So Ted and I took objects — a wooden truck, a ball of twine, a rock and a velvet box — and put both hands on the one we chose to feel. We closed our eyes and felt over the object with the right hand, then the left hand; then we looked, carefully, at each detail, and closed our eyes again to feel once more. We pressed the object firmly, pinched it, touched it gently; we noted mentally and verbally the shape, the size, the direction of any rib or pooch, corner or flat in the surface.

Next, we felt with seperate fingers in the same way. It took a couple of months to separate the fingers and feel with them accurately. We also felt objects with other parts of the body — the feet, the elbows, the shoulders, the back, the cheeks, the lips, always making sure we knew the left from the right hand side of the body we were using and the left from the right side of the object we were touching. When the horizontal direction was established we advanced into knowing what went up and down or in and out.

At last the visual image retained behind the closed lids became clear and accurate when either constructed by simply the feel of an object or the sight of it, so clear, in fact, that we could hold the visual image in mind while looking at the object and compare the two images. Then we transferred from objects to pictures.

We looked at a picture, closed the eyes and held the memory of it that we might judge the distance of one representation in the

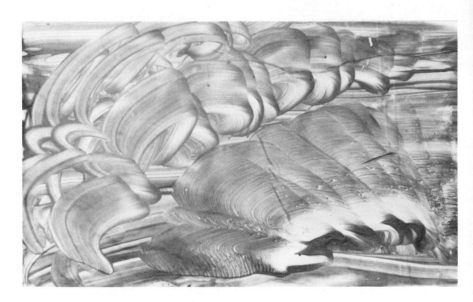

Andy's red-orange finger painting of a storm — hand dominance established through finger-painting.

picture from the other. We learned about foreground and background, comparison of sizes and of color, its intensity, shade or tint, and of differences and likenesses in the same picture or from one picture to another.

Finally, Ted was able, in about four months, to *imagine* the feel, *approximate* the shape and *judge* the tint or shade of color in a bowl of fruit with enough accuracy to make a good drawing of it with colored chalk. He was ecstatic.

So was his mother. He had begun to read.

I have found that some children's hand dominance was established from fingerpainting — in using not only the hand and fingers in the paint but arms and, in some instances, faces, as well; and, invariably, the ability to read also appeared. Reading began with one child after he learned to model figures in clay.

The kind of relaxation resident in tactual activities, which employ cooperative nerve-muscle-senses as a unit, seems to open the avenues of intake and liberate submerged potentials. Considering the tremendous role the senses play in the process of learning, probably the most important thing we could do right here is to devote the next section to an examination of their development and use.

5. Closing the Gap

THE EDUCATIVE USE of the five senses to promote the NH Child's development is also a cardinal measure in rounding out his attitude about himself. Often, because of his injury, one or more of his sense systems remain locked in the primitive stages of man's evolutionary growth, causing parents and teachers to panic when he fails to mature in a particular performance. Therefore, to close the gap between effective and ineffective performance, it is necessary to bring the primitively operating sense system into the active present.

Quite by chance, as in Ted's case, I stumbled onto ways that have stimulated, organized or redirected sense responses into contemporary effectiveness. The results are always unique.

Johnny Wood gave no response whatever to pinpricking, slapping, pinching or biting on any part of his body that was tested. And there were added deficiencies, such as: lack of memory, inability to learn, sleeplessness and a constant impulse to eat. For these, he was brought to me.

His round cherubic face wore a concerned, dejected expression, and his round puffy figure slumped along in accord. The morning we met I asked him what had happened to make him feel sad.

"I don't feel sad, and I don't feel glad," he said.

"Then, you just naturally feel like a worm today," I prodded, hoping it would lead somewhere.

"I don't know what a worm feels like, but I think I'd like to be a worm."

"Really?" I was delighted. "Then, let's be worms."

The rug in the room was soft and fluffy, so we squirmed over the floor like worms. After a few squirms, Johnny took off his shirt and, as he rubbed over the soft rug, a contented look came into his face. "Does it feel good, John?" I asked.

"M-m-m."

"You *can* feel it?"

"Huh-huh."

"Tell me how it feels."

"Good. Good and warm."

"Would you like some good warm on top of you, too?"

"Huh-huh."

I took a roll of cotton and spread it over him. "Now, close your eyes," I told him, "so you can feel this good warm in every part of you while you squirm through it." And I held the cotton against his skin, as if he crawled through a small tube of softness — simulating for him a smooth worm hole in the earth . . . or, perhaps, prenatal containment.

Every day when he came to my house for our time together he wanted to squirm through the cotton. Then, one day, after our relaxation, he crawled under the cotton and went to sleep. Thereafter, he often went to sleep under the cotton. And a short time later his mother reported that he was sleeping at home in a manner considered more normal.

When the squirming lost its charm, we took to exercising the legs and arms, balancing with one foot on a wooden block and the other outstretched, walking a two-by-four, chinning and push-ups, lying flat and bringing ourselves to an upright position without touching hands. In this we exercised to *feel* the muscles, work them and control them until his body looked and acted as if it were animated with youthful energy. Somewhere during this process he took to learning and remembering, first through the *feel* in his fingers, then with eyes and ears.

He fully regained tactual response over his body, even to a degree of being quite sensitive, and he proved himself to be several points above normal in all other areas, as well. But why it happened thus, still waits for utterance.

After Johnny Wood I did a consistent amount of experimenting in the tactual area. I found that once a response is elicited it can be developed by using the opposite, such as: if cotton is used — as with Johnny — then use sandpaper, or just sand; after hot or cold water, use hot or cold air. The initial response can also be expanded by chain reaction, as: start with soft mud or any slimy material and follow that experience with fingerpaints which add color, then thick pudding used as fingerpaints to combine an experience with texture, color, taste, and smell. The combination of materials is unlimited.

Each added element in these combinations gives the sense so stimulated an added opportunity to exercise cooperation and brings the child's vehicles for learning nearer present day expectancy in acquiring knowledge. Further, as the delayed sense system responds and grows under these created exercises, as it moves close to maturity, a strange and unaccountable thing always seems to occur. All at once, all five senses fall into line, as if a missing cog suddenly fell into place; then each takes its functioning position and they operate as a unit, supporting one another intelligently and effectively.

When this happens, children I have had who must taste and smell each thing to find out what it is, now are able to recognize the object or material by sight or hearing or feel. Other children who had to feel objects, as if they were blind, though their reports stated that the eye structure appeared normal, began looking and seeing. Reversals of all kinds — in sight, hearing, handedness — have suddenly righted themselves. Then, these children began learning, and remembering.

Let me make it clear, no conclusive statement concerning these individual occurrences is here intended. Such a statement waits on scientific research and medical pronouncement. Yet, in working with the NH Child we are forced by necessity to use anything that works for his benefit, whether we know of its source or actual character or not. And to recount the occurrences does not constitute an attempt at scientific approximation.

Probably, creative exercises in the sensory region work because they are fun, as much as anything. And deeply gratifying. Tasting things is even more fun than feeling. Tasting different kinds of dirt, for instance, or salt, or soaked jelly beans. Tasting sweet things, sour things, tart things, sharp things, hot and cold things. A favorite is chocolate covered bitter root.

Children love becoming expert in detecting the differences in texture, flavors, combinations, food characteristics and taste associations. This sense is greatly fortified by feeling, smell and visualization.

The sense of smell in our culture, with our deodorizers and effluvia tabus, has suffered from excess refinement. All of living prospers under contrasting impacts to strengthen and make flexible. And when one sense is weakened for lack of such impact, the whole sensory unit is weakened and often falls apart.

Like primitive man, children revel in the smell of their own dirty bodies, of the excrement, of sharp reactions to putrid decay and sticky sweetness. Though they wrinkle their noses, they like it. And they should have the opportunity to experience olfactory contrasts and to evaluate them.

One day I used fragrances and offensive odors with a group of ten and eleven year olds to create a complete dramatic experience:

For some weeks we had been sharpening the sense of smell; then the children declared they were ready for more penetrating experiments. We relaxed, sitting up, closed our eyes and remained quiet for a moment. That moment of quiet preparation within oneself is essential for sensitive response and interpretation.

While everyone was quiet I passed a damp mildewed rag under each nose. "What does that make you think of?" I asked.

"The garbage can . . . a dirty old wet towel . . . the bathroom after pop's been in there . . . the smell under a rock that has been on the damp ground for a long time."

"When you lift up the rock?"

"Yes."

"All right, each of us will lift up a rock that has been on damp ground for a long, long time. Can you feel it in your hand?"

"Yes."

"Can you smell the damp ground?"

"Yes."

"Now, look at the ground. What do you see in that place where the rock was?"

"Dirt . . . holes where worms live . . . a lot of little bugs running around . . ."

"Can all of you see the little bugs running?" I asked.

"Yes."

"What do they look like?"

"Kind of flat and black . . . with thin wings . . . and gold spots on them . . ."

"Here, smell them," I said, and held out a bit of half dried linseed oil under each nose. "Smell carefully. Now, still keep your eyes closed, but get down on the damp ground and try to catch a bug."

Eyes shut tight, they scrambled onto the floor and scurried here and there, until each caught a bug. "Smell your hands," I said. "What do you smell?"

"Bug smell!" they cried, surprised that the odor could be brought out of memory when no actual odor was present.

"Now, this is a new smell . . . the wind is bringing a new smell," I told them, as I waved a burning twig of Juniper in the air. "What is it?"

"It's the guardian of the forest!" one child cried. The others nodded. A couple drew in a quick awed breath.

"We didn't hurt the bugs, O Mighty One," the least imaginative child in the group pleaded earnestly. "We will let them go."

"We will let them go," everyone agreed. And each opened his hands to let the bugs run away.

Just then I squeezed a puff or two of wood violet talc over their heads without any comment. "Flowers are blooming," one said. "The guardian of the forest is thanking us," said another.

"Then it is time to stop and go home," I said.

This experience proved to be a turning point for some of these children. One little girl who had always played by herself began relating to others in the group. Another began painting at the easel, something she had refused to do before. A series of very revealing pictures resulted that helped us understand her better. One of the boys found he could concentrate after the prolonged focus on scent, and effectively brought his new skill to bear in learning to read and spell. Another fellow was able to relax the muscles in the back of his throat and release tensions that caused a strident nasality in his speech.

Experiences that become turning points in a child's life are, of course, the product of a succession of meaningful impressions; and we have no way of knowing just which one will catapult inward change into concrete expression. The teacher, however, always wonders if other responses of the group had been chosen on which to expand the experience, would more have been able to reach a turning point? It seems that we have to choose that which appears best for the group as a whole at the moment, and trust. One day, when maturity approaches that level, the choice will fall upon the child, then *he* will have to be helped to trust the results without quibbling.

At these turning points the child's attitude about himself undergoes some significant reorganizing. Important segments of his self-image slide into place and to his surprise and delight he finds he is a "can do," instead of a "can not," human organism. Development in hearing awareness is one of the most rewarding areas for significant reorganizing. I have had such sudden results that the child himself was startled.

Bonny, seven, had never talked, and was supposed deaf. Yet, she had the happy animated face of a hearing child. So, after gaining her cooperation and determining by means of a few simple games that she was left handed and left footed, we started out upon a little experimentation.

She had taken up a small wooden pop-gun and we were, by turns hitting each other in the palm of the hand with the cork that popped out. She showed delight, without laughing or making any vocal accompaniment to pleasure; she merely popped the gun and beamed.

I took a small cardboard cylinder from the inside of a roll of toilet tissue and pressed it close to her left ear. (I chose the left ear because of the left hand and foot preference.) Then, I spoke the word "pop" into the cardboard cylinder with as much resonance as I could produce. The vibratory effect of the sound going through that length and type of cardboard tingled in my hand that held the cylinder and up my arm, as it must have tingled also through her ear.

Bonny turned and looked at me, startled. Then she put her ear forward for the cardboard to touch it again. I spoke into the cylinder once more . . . *and she replied,* "POP!" The first word she had ever spoken.

In a month we had a list of twenty-five words that she was using. After a time, we discarded the cylinder.

There were children who seemed to hear well enough so they talked and screamed and whispered accurately when directed, but they could not sing nor determine whether one tone was higher or lower than another, or identify a tune. Yet many of them learned to sing by prostrating their faces and whole body over the wooden sounding frame of a piano while it was being played at immoderate volume. After a time they were able to detect and respond to very delicate tones.

Others learned to sing by holding a plucked tuning fork in the open mouth and modifying the tones by the movement of the mouth. Such stimulation is also very effective with the NH Child whose hearing intake and output is undeveloped. Talking or singing into a coffee can, used as a resonating chamber with the hands held tightly at the base of the can to receive the vibration, also stimulates and establishes hearing in the deeper and broader areas of awareness. Clapping the hands sharply, with a group, to different rhythms, stamping the feet or beating the body with the fists to rhythm and change of pitch often brings a response where nothing else will. Having partners take turns beating each other down the back with their fists while the one beaten holds a vocal tone is a great deal of fun and generally productive.

Then, there are all sorts of instruments to use, such as the deep voiced gong I tried with Sid whose hearing skipped and blanked out and confounded him like some wily phantom.

Though Sid was only nine, he was taller than I am, and built like stone blocks, solid and unyielding. He had small bright grey eyes and the odd expression of seeing far away, but conscious of nothing under his feet. His speech followed this same pattern, vague and uncommunicative, mostly incomplete sentences and parts of words. Fortunately, he was mild tempered and wanted to be cooperative.

Besides building on his other basic needs, we began testing through the hearing regions looking for a fruitful response. He seemed to get a great deal from shattering glass or the cracking sound of a golf ball hitting on cement; then we tried the sound and flash of two electric wires touched together and the striking of a heavy hammer on metal, as well as the cry of animals in pain or fright played on a record. Yet, none of these made the right contact.

At last I brought out a large gong, borrowed from a friend who had lived in the Islands. It turned the trick. Sid was lifted into a sort of seventh heaven where he could have listened to the reverberations of the gong hour after hour, scarcely moving. Even with the gong put away while he worked on something else, he would say, all at once, "I'm hearing the gong."

This developing memory in the ear was affecting memory in all areas.

One day he struck the gong and listened with the customary serene expression on his face. "Close your eyes," I said, "and make a picture of the sound." After a moment, I asked, "What does it look like?"

"Waves," he answered. This was a thrilling moment. His imagination had been tapped.

"What color are the waves?"

"Blue, up close. Then green. Then yellow and orange. There's a little red . . . and far, far away . . . it is all white."

"Go with them as far as you can," I said, wondering and hoping as to the outcome of this suggestion. In a little while, I asked, "What do you see now?"

"Spots, like cotton on fire whirling around. Some are big and some little."

"What do you think they are?"

"Stars. There's a big one."

"Could it be Jupiter?"

"I don't know. But I see people. Funny looking. They've got square heads and round bodies that look like flowers."

"You mean they have clothes on that look like flowers?"

He shook his head. "No, that's what they're made of. Now, they're going down in some holes in the ground. They're waving at me. They want me to come, too."

"Are you going?"

"No, I'll go some other time."

With his imagination awakened, the gates of learning opened for Sid. There was still a great deal of work to be done to establish accurate listening habits, but they came as we pursued the study of Jupiter and other planets, creating new and unusual sounds which might be heard in these strange and different places. When we began exploring the language skills, we also created different sounding words and new rhythms in speech which might come from outer space, then, bit by bit all academic achievement eased into function.

Sid taught me something that I had never thought of before and have never heard discussed anywhere, yet it certainly should be. It concerns giving instructions to children, or adults, but most emphatically giving instructions to an NH Child.

Teachers say . . . and I have said the same myself . . . "Please, copy the sentences on the board and put your paper on my desk when you have finished." Such an instruction sounds simple and direct, on the surface. However, on close scrutiny, most inquirers would admit there were two sections in the direction, never dreaming that to the majority of children, and particularly to the NH, there are *seven* separate directions — four implied and three voiced.

Because the neurologically impaired are so intuitively aware, implied instructions, or ideas, are more direct and impelling than voiced ones. With many, as with Sid, the voiced statements muddle and scramble through the implied so that no sense can be made of them anyway.

However, for the moment, he has yielded himself to your leadership and tries to make something of what you have said, yet he is caught, and immobilized, between the strong implied impressions, running one on top of the other, and the half heard words spoken. You must voice one section of the instruction, then wait, giving the listener an opportunity to act upon what was heard, as (illustrating with the above mentioned direction):

1. Take a sheet of paper . . . (wait for him to get it)

2. Put it on your desk . . . (wait)

3. Take a pencil . . . (or a pen)

4. Look at the sentences on the board . . . (read together)

5. Copy these sentences on the paper . . . (give time)

6. Are you almost finished? . . . (forewarning)

7. All right, now put your paper on my desk.

Not many people, thought to be perfectly normal, can follow a double or triple direction clearly. They either stop and stare at the instructor for a minute or two to get a bearing on where to begin, or start off quickly and end up forgetting half of what was expected.

But anyone, together with the NH, can *learn* to take even very complicated directions. And it is a matter of learning, listening intently, organizing consecutively, step by step, and teaching the mind to hold to the job until it is finished. I have had children who became able to hold in mind twelve or fifteen sections of an instruction before beginning to act, and carry them through perfectly.

Another dimension in listening is the function known as "hearing with the inner ear." The use of this inner hearing is essential to the creation, and full interpretation, of music, as well as of the spoken word. The dramatist makes use of this faculty in conceiving and writing a play, in the same manner that a musician composes dialogue between instruments.

It seems logical, to me, that a distinction should be made between "inner hearing" and "intuitive hearing." In the first function, the hearing of inner sounds is touched off by a given sound, a verbal suggestion that creates an image — sensory, visual or auditory — or by any experience that creates such an image, and any augmentation of inner hearing that follows the initial stimulation develops in a sequential series of images, one created out of the other. This, I have done many times with children and adults for the purpose of maturing deeper and richer listening and exercising the imagination. An incident with Jack Romer illustrates:

Jack, age eleven, and I had tried a number of exercises in extended hearing — playing half a scale and supplying the other half by auditory memory, or striking a tone and supplying the same tone an octave higher, or by hearing a raucous sound and creating the tonal opposite. Then we decided to try purely inner hearing.

There were two doors that led into a hallway. At one door Jack sat facing me with his ear to the keyhole and I sat at the other, ear to keyhole. We listened into the blank silence for some time, our hearing seemingly protruded through the keyholes, alert, expectant.

Then I lifted my fist and pretended to beat the palm of my other hand, though actually making no sound. "What could that sound like?" I whispered softly.

"A man stomping down the hall."

"Can you really hear him?"

"Yes."

"What is he doing now?"

"Opening the outside door."

"What now?"

"I smell the air from the outdoors."

"What do you hear?"

"A bird singing."

"Sing the song the bird is singing." He sang three sweet notes. They were very similar to bird notes, yet not a song that I had ever heard. "Do you hear anything else besides the bird singing?" I asked.

Jack listened intently. "Yes, someone is saying that was a nice song. Sing it again."

"Can you sing it again?" He sang the three notes just as before. "Can you sing it three tones higher?"

He sang it higher. "Can you sing it three tones lower?" I asked him.

Jack tried, then said, "No, I can't."

"Try the song once more as the bird sang it," I urged. Jack sang it true to pitch and rhythm as he had the first time. "Now, try it three tones lower," I said. And he sang it.

"What kind of a musical instrument could play that song and sound very much like the bird?"

"A violin."

"When you sang very low just then, what kind of an instrument could sound like that?"

"A big violin."

"Can you hear the small violin playing the song?"

"Yes."

"Now, listen again to the big violin playing the song." He listened. "Can you hear it clearly?" I asked.

"Yes."

"Listen to the big violin playing just one of the notes in the song over and over. Hear it?"

"Yes."

"Let it begin to fade away . . . farther and farther . . . far into the distance. What does it sound like now?"

"A fog horn."

"That's fine. Do you think if we played this game again sometime that you could bring back the sound of the fog horn and the bird song?"

"Yes."

"Listen a minute to the fog horn. Hear it?"

"Yes."

"Now, listen to the bird. Hear it clearly?"

"Yes."

"Remember them so you can bring them back some day. Maybe you could put them together to make a different song. Do you think so?"

"Maybe."

A week or two later we tried recalling these two sounds and found them firmly imbedded in memory. Subjoined to this memory was increased auditory awareness, such as: an ability to hear and follow directions more accurately, to consciously turn off the hearing when concentrating, and to choose and organize and evaluate meaningful sounds from the contiguous barrage of sounds present in our modern living. No doubt this experience accounts in some measure for the fact that Jack elected to compose our Christmas song that year to accompany our play. Such is often the result when inner hearing is augmented.

On the other hand, "intuitive hearing" seems out of reach of conscious development or augmentation. At least, I have never been able to touch or stimulate it in another person. It apparently acts thus: helpful and creative knowledge appears in the consciousness without announcement, connective lead-in or association with accepted logic. Yet the knowledge invariably adds a necessary element to whatever thinking is at hand, often reveals something entirely new.

Intuitive factors resident in the senses will be discussed more in detail a little later. At the moment, it is important to explore the sense of sight, the lead sense.

Modern man places an unequal burden on sight, expecting incredible performance from it, unmindful of its dependence on a strong and reliable performance from the other senses for adequate efficiency. It is to be hoped that the primitive deviations in sight presented by the NH Child will quicken research in the function and use of this precious faculty. Present knowledge fails to meet the need of the child with an eye dysfunction that registers fragments of images.

Early man saw only parts of what we consider the whole of anything, as the NH Child with perceptual difficulties. Likewise, who is to say that what we see, called the whole image, might not be only a small part of a greater image?

Cave men caught sight of objects in motion — a bird in flight, a rodent running for cover — and lost sight of them when they ceased to move. Anything in motion attracts the eye of most children, especially the NH. And how many adults will watch a janitor adjusting a chair in back of a speaker instead of holding our attention on the person giving ideas?

Apparently, red was the first color to come into focus, a color eminently preferred by primitives and NH children. There are those who see no color at all.

Once, with a child who saw no color, I took a piece of dull black paper and held it in a spot where diffused light was evenly distributed. He was to squint his eyes, look steadily at the paper, then open his eyes suddenly. Doing this, he was able to see red spots against the black paper. We practiced seeing these red spots until they became distinct enough to compare with red objects, in diffused light first, then in ordinary lighting. When red was clearly established in the child's eye perception, he was instructed to look at the red steadily, then close his eyes; in this manner green, the compliment of red, appeared. Time was taken to establish a perception of green, after which glass jars of yellow and blue water paint were placed on either side of a green one. By blending blue and yellow, many times, to make green, gradually the two new colors came into perceptive focus and the child was no longer color primitive.

With a little girl, named Mary Lou, who saw only bits and pieces here and there, we did some interesting things which brought her sight into the active present. And we had a great deal of fun doing it.

Mary Lou was only five when she came into our working association. She was a darling, ash blonde with pale skin and large brown eyes, and a good mind.

One of the first objects we used to play with was a peg-board where the pegs were pounded into the board with a wooden mallet after placing the peg in the hole with the hand. She had great difficulty putting the peg in the hole, so we took to the shut-eye routine. We did the whole operation with eyes closed, carefully and slowly at first, my hand guiding, then letting her be on her own.

At last I said, "Now, Mary Lou, look at the peg in your hand before you close your eyes and feel it. Now, look at the hole, then feel it. *Now, watch* the peg and the hole come together. Can you see both of them?"

When she was able to follow each separate operation, seeing with eyes and with feeling, we put the whole together. We counted each peg we put in and after they were in we counted them again, touching and seeing. To this we added objects made with toy builders, take-apart toys and building blocks, bit by bit becoming the whole, then taking it apart again.

The day finally came when she was able to create a visual image and describe it from the touch or from the sight. (When the eye and the hand become partners they form an infallible team whose coordinate action underwrites a number of other coordinations, mental and physical.)

Now, Mary Lou learned about the right side and the left side, the top and bottom of herself and other objects, the foreground and the background of herself, of a view or of a picture, and comparative sizes, shapes and colors. So we were ready to extend these images into imaginative creations, or "inner seeing."

We took three wooden blocks — a cube, a pyramid and a sphere, with which we were familiar by sight and feeling and mental image. These shapes were placed on a table, the pyramid on the right hand, the sphere on a pedestal in the middle and the cone on the left.

"Close your eyes, Mary Lou," I said. "Can you see the blocks in front of you?" When she nodded, I told her to touch them to make sure she was seeing the right shape in the right place. "Now," I said, "take your hands away and let's see the ball turning around all by itself. Can you see it turning?"

"It's doing it," she said.

"All right. Make it turn around the other way."

"It's doing it."

"Good. Now, make the square block turn around and around."

When she had the cube turning, we set the pyramid moving around. That she could see — perceive — these three objects in motion at the same time and hold them in consciousness attested to a probable attainment of our goal for her sight. But we should go farther. I believe it has wisely been said that we should always "over-learn."

"Mary Lou, while these blocks are turning, do you suppose you could make the ball bounce up in the air?"

"Yes, it's doing it," she replied.

"Fine. Now, have the ball stay on the pedestal and let the block with the sharp point jump up in the air."

"It's doing it."

"Is it turning around as it jumps up?"

"Yes."

"Are the other two blocks still turning, too?"

"Yes."

"Good. Have the pointed block jump up in the air and then come down on the top of the square block."

"It did it."

"Now, have the square block and the pointed block jump up together and come down on the right side of the ball."

"They did."

"All right. Let's make the ball a yellow color . . ."

After each block was given a color, we repeated the act of turning and jumping; then we changed colors and after that we changed shapes — cutting the ball in half, making a hole through the cube, cutting the pyramid in two and putting the bottom half on the top. At last we pretended the blocks were made of rubber and stretched them up and down and out at the sides and in at the middle.

How Mary Lou laughed! And how completely her seeing became whole!

The sixth sense is the great synthesizer, common sense, that transposes all the data received by the brain from the five physical inlets into what is called reason or good sense or logic. Most NH children are weak in this important area. For a time, they are obliged to accept and follow a pattern of reason and good judgment given them by those who love and guide them. If the child is gotten young, this is not difficult; but each added year makes its added demand upon patience and understanding, upon ingenuity and persistent determined effort.

I have found that learning to use the typewriter aids in synthesizing the intake from the five senses. The control of separate fingers, the touch of the keys, the sound — kept in rhythm — with the touch and the sight of the letters on the chart, all of which grows into holding a visualized idea in mind for expression through the coordinated channels. When the skill finally develops into writing stories and plays, as well as poetry, synthesizing common sense has come into bloom. I have also found that having a child choose a play which fits a group, then select the children who rightly fit the characters and direct the action as *"reason in human behavior"* — brought down to child terms — never fails to aid and develop common sense.

Now, there is a seventh sense, intuition. Previously, we spoke of it as a helpful and creative knowledge that appears in the consciousness without announcement, connective lead-in or association with any element of logic. And, it is to be added, the NH Child, more often than not, operates fully in this area.

While I have never found a means of augmenting or stimulating this faculty in another person, I have been able to make use of it to advance the cause of common sense. For example:

Johnny Wood, the boy whose tactile sense was supposedly missing, always knew before he arrived in the morning what surprise awaited him for work well done. By analyzing the purpose and reason for the surprise and applying that same reasoning to the forethinking put into the plans, carried out sequentially, step by step, for his self-development, he began helping me plan what step logically follows the one we had just completed.

Sid, when crossed in some desired intention or reprimanded for some unacceptable act, would blow up into a wild temper even while, at the same time, he knew, intuitively, without a whit of reasoning in his knowing, the rightness of his being thwarted. Step by step we brought reasons for the rightness of limitations into his understanding and this helped him to use logic in situations of all kinds, preserving his naturally mild nature and his bend toward peace-making.

Then, there was little Betty Ann, five, with multiple problems, two of which would prevent her from learning to read for quite some time, who was able to name the titles on a stack of phonograph records she had never seen before simply by putting her hand on them.

And there was Jack Mullen with no knowledge of mathematics, numerals or computations, in fact he could not even count, who could give the answer instantly to any math problem presented to him orally.

All very young children know intuitively what those around them are thinking and feeling, where to look for things hidden from them and how best to "appeal" for something they want. This intuitive faculty disappears as reason and common sense take over. So it is with the NH Child, in whom the faculty perseverates to serve him until the mind faculty matures.

Do we regret the loss of the seventh sense which we have assisted out of action? Or do we rejoice that because of its perseveration in NH children and our recognition of its effect and function, the groundwork might be prepared for its permanent use in the evolutionary plan?

Now, with the use of his senses at his command, the NH Child faces his future with an entirely new expectation. Once his self-image is complete, understandable and controllable, he is ready to challenge the not-self.

6. Educate to Concentrate

$\mathbb{T}$HE THIRD BASIC principle is *to educate* the Child. Up to this point we have coordinated attitudes and trained the vehicles for learning; now, using these prepared channels, we *lead out, draw out, unfold* and *develop.* Such a procedure implies that that which is to be led out and developed lies within waiting to be released and directed into meaningful, as well as useful, objectives, an implication that restates the pure meaning of education.

Very little "instruction" is effective with NH children. *To instruct* means "to put in something that is lacking," "to fill a void," implying that mental growth is effected from without by an authority who selects and organizes the material to fill the void. By such a procedure the student must be wise enough and mature enough to transform that material into the energizing elements on which the mind can grow and develop. Many children find this *act of transforming* impossible of achievement, among them the neurologically impaired. So, we *educate.*

The ways and means, methods and techniques by which to educate are created *en passant* by the child and the teacher together, without the slightest intention that these means will be of interest or use to any other child. In a few instances, the same technique works with one or two others, and, if streamlined to fit special needs, might even work with a number of cases, providing the technique is a fundamental one. However, a well founded practice is to expect that the methods used with a child at the moment, are effective only for the moment, and serve as an example of what *can* be done when the right means come into exercise at the right moment, with the right child.

What of the teacher who has been taught to rely on set, prescribed methods and techniques, who feels naked and afraid without them?

That teacher must relax and let the excitement of exploring and growing with the child take over. I always go into a situation fully armed with all the techniques and methods I have ever known or can think of — just in case — but with the determination to throw them all out the window the minute the child makes an overture that I can use and develop. And he never fails to make a revealing overture, either a negative or a positive one. Either can be explored. Either can prove fruitful.

Jim Beldon was fifteen years old, a ward of the Juvenile Court, one of a small number accepted by the Children's Educational Theater in Seattle for participation in its various activities hoping to serve as a link in the boys' rehabilitation. I helped out as one of the directors in the Theater.

Jim was a husky fellow, handsome and dark, an inveterate stutterer and a consummate braggart. Though the court records were not available to us, it was not hard to guess what kind of trouble he featured. A youngster who boasts of making five hundred a week — and probably made a third of that — yet read at a primer level and could scarcely write his name, carried his own label.

What to do with him in the Theater was a problem. He was useless in stagecraft. He spilled more paint than he used, could not hit a nail on the head or judge his own strength in stretching muslin on flats. After making the rounds of all the departments, he finally arrived in mine where we were rehearsing the play SILVER THREAD, the story of a miner boy who faced his fear and saved a Princess.

I let him drift around a bit while I wondered what in the world to try him on: keep count of the costumes, or guard the borrowed properties? Then one day I watched him bullying the other boys in the cast, swaggering in front of the girls when the boys cringed and acting like a monster who tried to suck their blood.

"Jim," I said, "how would you like to have the part of good King Radnor in the play? You are about the right size."

Taken by surprise, he stared at me for a moment; then I saw that he was about to laugh in my face. To avoid such a possibility in front of a gaping audience, I hurried him into my office. There, he slumped on a chair and burst into tears.

Jim not only carried the part of King Radnor, without a flaw in diction or character, for twelve splendid performances but took the male lead in our next production of REBECCA OF SUNNYBROOK FARM. Then, after two years in the Children's Theater, he went on to school and became a radio announcer.

The means which helped Jim to learn character portrayal and clear expressive speech came about as unpremeditated as his selection for a part in the first place. It was a matter of expedience, because I lacked the time to work individually with him enough to be effective, his need for special help being so pronounced, that I asked a co-worker in the Theater, a retired actor, to speak the lines for him as they should be spoken so Jim could learn to react bodily, instantly, to the meaning embodied in the words. This he learned to do, like a marionette, the strings operating him being the color and inflection in the speaker's voice.

After practicing hour on hour for three months this way, he stepped on stage one day during rehearsal, opened his mouth and spoke his own lines in the same expressive tones and rhythm his mentor had used. By listening and practicing Jim's whole muscle-nerve pattern had been reorganized, even his facial expression had changed entirely, his mental attitude had become refocussed and it gradually infiltrated his daily living. Yet, in spite of the success of this method with Jim, I have never used it with anyone else. I have never found another child for whom I felt it was fitted.

However, the basic premise in the ways and means which came about for Corky Manning, a student whose first revealing overture was a positive one, has served many children. Corky was enrolled in one of the schools where I served as a special teacher. The vice-principal spoke to me about him. "There is a boy in the Sixth Grade," she said, "who has not learned to read or write, though I think he could learn if someone knew what to do for him. Would you talk with him and see what you think?"

This was most surprising. At that time school personnel usually dismissed a child who could not accomplish with a blanket opinion that he was uneducable. So I looked forward to meeting Corky with a fervent prayer that I be able to do something for him.

My heart went out to the tall blond boy that slipped quietly into my office and sat down as unobtrusively as a spot of dust settling into a corner. Such a handsome, finely built boy. I turned and looked out the window to spare him the humiliation of my gaze.

When I turned back I caught his long sensitive fingers moving over the keys on my typewriter sitting on the table beside him. Seeing my eyes on him, he quickly withdrew his hand.

"Do you type?" I asked.

He shook his head.

"Would you like to?"

He nodded.

"Mrs. Duarte, the vice-principal, tells me you are quite a mechanic," I said.

"Yes, I can fix most anything. My dad has bought me a lot of good tools." His voice was strong and well-modulated, disavowing his shrinking behavior.

"Then, with such well trained hands, typing should be easy for you," I assured him. "Sit around to the machine and let's take a swing at it."

He pulled his chair around to the typewriter and I showed him how to place his fingers on the keys. Suddenly he drew back, as if something hit him in the face. "Those keys," he said, indicating the left side of the keyboard. "They come right at me."

So I offered to type anything we wanted to talk about until we found out what was causing the condition with his eyes and what to do for it. Two weeks later we had a report from the occulist, the most highly recommended eye specialist in the county, which included a modern, thriving city. There was a letter to me with the report which read:

"When will you teachers learn how to teach children to read? I'm getting mighty tired of having teachers send children to me for tests in an effort to cover up their own deficiencies. There is nothing wrong with this boy's eyes. All he needs is someone who can teach him."

Of course, he was right, but not in the way he meant. And I did some long and earnest contemplation on how to teach Corky.

At our next meeting I said, "Corky, you know we don't have to look at the keyboard at all to type. We can teach our fingers to touch the keys that we hold in mind. Do you know the written alphabet?"

"No."

"Then, we'll learn it from the sound and the feel of what we want to say."

Laboriously we went through the process of listening to the thing we said, letter by letter, and punching the corresponding key on the typewriter. This worked fine, and he was delighted, until he achieved skill enough to attempt long sentences and complicated words spelled unphonetically. Now we had to learn to visually use the symbols. Corky's sense of sight must take its place with his other trained vehicles for learning.

With letters cut from sandpaper, we traced them — using index and middle fingers — first with eyes closed, then with eyes open, listening and feeling, feeling and looking. Then we made words and traced in the same way until we could see the whole word clearly with eyes shut. Next, we placed felt letters on the typewriter keys, letting the fingers which had become familiar with the letter position by sound now stimulate a visual image from the feel of the letter form.

At last, we let all of these measures fade into the background and learned to *concentrate* on the thought to be expressed in the written symbols, first a short sentence, then a long one and finally a complete paragraph, visualizing the finished paragraph and reading it off at the end. And, one day, after these periods of concentration, Corky began reading from books.

When he was seventeen, he invented a compression brake for bicycles, the returns from which insured his college education.

I always learn as much as the child. With Corky I learned that concentration is an essential for the release and use of the creative potential in effective education; and it has grown with me over the years. Some implications in the use of concentration have been discussed previously in connection with various points of training for the NH Child, but let us concern ourselves with it briefly because of its significance in the educative process.

Dr. C. Guy Suits, describing the coherent light known as laser — Light Amplification by Stimulated Emission of Radiation, states: "Energy emitted by most light sources might be compared to a crowd of schoolboys running willy-nilly out the schoolhouse door when the bell rings at the end of day. With coherent light, the energy is like a troup of well-trained soldiers, marching in perfect step along an absolutely straight line." He goes on to say that coherent light concentrated through a laser becomes tens of thousands of times more powerful than the electro-magnetic waves now in use in transmitting information, or performing a hundred other miraculous tasks.

I see an analogy here between light energy and thought energy. Concentrated thought energy is a thousand times over more effective than that same energy allowed to flit willy-nilly. I am sure more people fail in utilizing their full potential from lack of concentration than from lack of capacity. And, again, I am sure that most people agree on this. Yet, where can you go for training in this essential skill?

Perhaps, the NH Child is the deviate which will trigger the awareness for a need in this direction for all children, because the great majority of neurologically impaired cannot tap their potentials at all without dynamic concentration. Once their potential is tapped, added effort is required in concentration to put it into effective, purposeful performance, each day pressing themselves to greater effort, fraction by fraction, past any previous level of fatigue. And, they must learn to like it, think it is fun, make it a contest with themselves.

Exercises for concentration can be simple and interesting, even fascinating:

First Lesson (Start in from this point each lesson.)

1. Relax thoroughly, either sitting or lying. When deep quiet is attained — say softly —

2. "Today we are going to start out on an adventure together. It will not be easy, but it will be fun. Now, tell yourself, deep inside, that it will be fun and that you will stay quiet and relaxed all the way to the end . . . Now, listen . . .

3. Strike a tone on a simple musical instrument.

4. "Did you hear that?" (Wait a minute, then strike again, and explain.) "That is called a tone. A musical tone. But we will just say a tone. How many times did you hear that tone?" (Strike again.) "You don't have to tell me, only tell yourself, so you *know*, how many times you hear the tone." (Strike one again.)

5. "Listen once more." (Strike twice, same tone.) "How many times did you hear it? Don't tell me, but tell yourself."

6. Strike the same tone three times, slowly. "How many times did you hear it that time?"

7. "Listen again to three tones." (Strike the three same tones.) "Now, listen . . ."

8. Strike the tones run as closely as possible into one. "Did they run together? Now see what they are doing?"

9. Strike the first time very firmly, the next softer and the last very softly. "What did the last tone do? Did it fade out very softly?"

10. "Now, listen again. Here is the first tone . . . (Strike) . . . here is the second tone . . . (Strike) . . . here is the last tone. Which one is the softest?" (Wait) "Have you decided which is the softest? Then which was the loudest? Which did I hit the hardest to make it sound loud?"

11. Decide carefully inside yourself. Take your time." (Wait) "Have you decided? That was a hard decision to make and some of you might not have been able to do it . . . so listen once more . . . this is the first tone . . . here is the second and . . . here is the last one. Which is the softest and which is the loudest?"

12. "Have you decided? Good. Now, just for fun count out loud with me each time I strike a tone . . . one, two, three, four . . . etc. (To ten with very young children, farther if they are older and you think they can.)

This very simple exercise, as you can readily see, has given a remarkable foundation on which to begin the NH Child's education . . . the leading out, the unfolding, the self-development:

(a) The attention has been concentrated on a single musical tone for eight to ten minutes, quite a beginning span of attention for distractible children. The development of concentration can be effective with small groups, too. More effective one-to-one, of course.

(b) Relaxation has been maintained (practiced) for eight to ten minutes also, after it had once been achieved. Thus the brain-nerve-muscle program of action is taught to reorganize as a cooperative vehicle for the mind. Thus the mind, too, finding a ready, yielding channel, becomes engaged in the outward flow, happily, for it is the tremendous drive in the mind's desire toward expression beating against the impassable barriers in the body that brings such conflict and confusion to the neurologically impaired. But once the body yields and the channels open and the flow begins, the mind energy, to be useful, must meet and coordinate with physical limitations and physical procedures The faculty called reason, operated by the skill called concentration, takes care of this meeting and coordinating between the mind and its vehicle, relating experiences from the outer senses to form judgments and conclusions for action. And, as we know, the majority of NH children find their greatest barrier at this point. Here is their greatest need for loving guidance.

(c) Note that in this initial lesson in concentration the purchase is laid for reason, inner judgment, one's own decisions. Taking ideas with which he *can* cope, the adventurer is led into simple, seemingly unimportant deductions and evaluations because it is pleasant, easy and unhurried, and no one asks him to stand up to acknowledge his shame if his conclsuion is different from someone else's, or if he have none at all. He is also introduced, with no unfair competition attached, to new vocabulary which he will meet again in reading and arithmetic, and their meaning made plain. Yet a phase of competition does appear at which he leaps like a trout to a fly, competition with himself. The guide suggests that someone else may not have gotten a "hard to understand" point, which he got immediately, and he has a chance to prove to himself that he got it. And the joy of self-development has begun for him.

(d) Medical and psychiatric advisors warn about, educators and teachers shun, and parents tremble at the use of pressure with their children. Yet the fact remains, and we as a race are having to face it, that learning just does not take place without pressure and discipline, the ordering and forming of our actions and thought according to an acceptable pattern. Where is this pressure and discipline to come from? Some are answering readily . . . *from within ourselves.* These are adults saying this who have experienced the hard lot of trying to discipline themselves after years of flitting about ineffectively. Are we to let our children waste the best parts of their lives as we have wasted ours without discipline? Or can we look at these exercises in concentration with new eyes? They *do* give the opportunity for creating and perfecting self-discipline, unconsciously at first, but consciously in the final stages.

(e) Let it be stated very clearly: no one has a corner on the ways and means of developing concentration; it is entirely a matter of individual needs and interest, even of philosophy. However, there are certain requirements for success: the teacher must be able to relax and concentrate in order to guide others in the skill, the point selected on which to concentrate must embody enough facets of interest for both teacher and child so its augmentation will be fruitful, and the exercises in concentration must be carried far enough and long enough to insure their permanent effectiveness.

Second Lesson (Repeat approach and main parts of First Lesson.)

1. Finish with the three strikes — hard, soft, softer — and the conclusion, and say softly, "Now, you are getting to be experts, an expert is someone who does things very well, and an expert keeps testing himself trying to do things better, always trying new adventures . . . so here we go on a new adventure ready to meet new friends . . . listen."

2. Strike four of the same tone used before. "How is this new friend different from the old one? Here is our old friend (Strike) . . . here is our new friend. (Strike four times) Did you hear the tone four times? This is Mr. Four."

3. "Are you very relaxed and easy? Test yourself . . . your head, arms, hands, loose legs . . . be sure you are very easy because Mr. Four is a tricky fellow and your ears have to be double sharp. Here he goes . . ." (Strike three of the same tone used before and the fourth two tones above.)

4. "What happened? Listen again" (Strike three the same and the last two tones above.) "Do you suppose you could tell yourself how many steps Mr. Four went up on the last tone?" (Strike four with the last tone *one* step above the other three.) "Here Mr. Four goes up one step on the last tone. "(Strike four with the last tone two steps above.) "Here he goes up two steps." (Strike four with the last tone three steps above.) "Here he goes *three* steps higher. Now, decide which this is . . . one step . . . two steps . . . or three steps." (Strike four with the last two tones above.)

5. "Listen again to what the three tones did for us" (Strike three — hard, soft, softer.) "Let's let the four tones do the same." (Strike hard, soft, softer.) "Oh, my, I have one tone left over. What shall I do with it? Shall I *add* it on at the last?" (Strike hard, soft, and two softer.) "Or shall I add it to the first tone?" (Strike two hard, soft, softer.) "Maybe we should add it in the middle, to the second tone." (Strike two in the soft.) "Which do you like the best?"

6. "Suppose we add that left over tone at the last and take it up two steps." (Strike hard, soft and two softer two steps above.) "Now, let's take it up just one step." (Strike) "Then three steps up." (Strike) "Which do you like best? One step up at the last . . ." (Strike) . . . "two steps up . . ." (Strike) . . . "or three steps?" (Strike)

7. "Listen . . ." (Strike the first two tones up two steps, the last two at the old placement.) "there we have the two high tones at the opposite end . . . in the beginning, instead of last. Listen again . . ." (Strike "there is the beginning . . . there is the ending . . . the last two tones."

8. "How would you like to hear our old friend again, only with the soft tone at the opposite end?" (Strike softest tone first; again the first tone softest but the hard tone two steps up.) "Tell yourself how that last three tones was different from the first three tones."

9. "Now, you really are experts. You have listened so well and made so many fine choices . . . you choose so well . . . it is such fun to choose for yourself . . . not easy, but fun. For our last testing, listen . . ." (Strike four, first high two steps, second low, third low, fourth high two steps.) "How was that different? Sing it out loud with me . . ." (Strike) "one, two, three, four . . . up, down, down, up . . . don't we have fun?"

This second lesson begins earnestly in forming the memory, the making of choices, the coming to decisions and conclusions, the recognizing of differences, and the experiencing of meanings in word and concept. From here the lessons should expand on these goals consistently adding the concepts of addition and subtraction — which has been started — multiplication and division, and other mathematical terms and processes; they should expand into physical concepts — sound, light, form, energy — their meaning, use, differences and likenesses, and their relationship to ourselves and our world, even our worlds. All these can be brought to the child through very simple mental exercises while he is relaxed, and concentration growing.

At about the tenth lesson, according to the manner in which you develop your central interest, visualization should be introduced actively. I say actively because some visualization may have been going on already, though it is doubtful. Most NH children have difficulty with visualization, so it must be guided from the most fundamental point. Visualization solidifies learning.

Tenth Lesson (Repeat relaxation approach.)

1. (Each child should have a box or bag of marbles and a slab of wood with grooves in which the marbles may be placed without rolling about. He or she may be on the floor or at a table where he can use a pencil and paper.) "Take a marble out of the box. Feel of it. Look at it. Put it in your mouth, if you want to, and let your mouth tell you how it is shaped. What do we call this shape? Yes, it is called *round*. While you have the marble in your

mouth, make your mouth round like the marble is round. Leave your mouth round but take out the marble. Now make a sound . . . O-O-O. That sound is called . . . O.

2. "Take your pencil. Make a picture on the paper of the sound called . . . O. It is just the same shape as the marble, isn't it? And this is the way we write . . . we write by making pictures of the sounds that come out of our mouths.

3. "Now, close your eyes. See the picture of the marble shape . . . the O sound . . . that you made on your paper. See it just as if you were looking at it with your eyes open. Can you see it? Open your eyes again and look. Look at the marble, look at its picture on the paper. Then close your eyes and see it. Feel the marble with your hands to help you see the picture clearer. Can you see it?

4. "Will you look inside yourself all over and be sure you are relaxed and easy? We are going to do something new and different and you must be easy so it can be fun. Hands and arms loose? Jaw loose, back and legs? Happy?

5. (Teacher takes a simple reed instrument) "Listen . . ." (Blow a single tone.) "Doesn't that sound very much like the O sound that comes out of our mouth when our mouth is round? Listen again . . ." (Blow) "When musicians write music they also make a picture shaped like a marble for each tone. Let's close our eyes and see the O sound picture each time this reed makes a tone." (Blow three tones, same placement.)

6. "Open your eyes. Take as many marbles out of the box as the tones you heard. Put the marbles in the grooves in your slab of wood. Listen to the tones once more." (Blow three.) "Do you have the same number of marbles? Put your finger on a marble each time you hear a tone." (Blow three.) "Did you have enough marbles? Don't tell me, just tell yourself."

7. "Now close your eyes and see the marbles. See your finger touching a marble each time you hear a tone." (Blow three.) "Did you do it? Good. Let's do it once more. See your finger touching a marble each time you hear a tone." (Blow four, same placement.) "Oh-oh, what happened? Were there enough marbles for each tone? Listen again. See the marbles. See your finger touching each one . . ." (Blow four.)

8. "Open your eyes and put your hand in the box. Take out as many marbles as you need for each tone you heard. Put

Cindy's expression of fragmentation. NH children have difficulty with visualizing themselves in relation to their environment.

Cindy's chalk expression of two animals correlating the O with circles in a body to get a likeness.

them beside the three marbles in the groove. Now touch the marbles with your finger . . . eyes open. Let's count out loud . . ." (Blow — one, two, three, four!)

9. "Take your pencil. Make a picture of the O sound each time you say it out loud. I will blow a tone each time you say the O." (Blow four.) "There. Now, close your eyes and see the four O's. See them? Good. That's it."

Visualization deals with the ability to see and feel form, all shapes and sizes and kinds of form and hold it in the mind's eye. It is the ability to see and judge the top and bottom of things, the slant and curve of lines, and the foreground and background . . . the far and near. Further, it relates to a well-established body image, which many children along with the NH do not have. Therefore, the lesson following the one just given should correlate the picture of the O with all the circles in the body. After that, establish the triangular shapes of the body, then the square and rectangular, to be followed by drawing one's portrait.

When the body image is whole, the visualization gained can then be extended successfully into the mental province of the imagination. Many instances have been cited during this whole discourse of the imagination having been awakened and used, of the necessity for activating the imagination as a final factor in bringing about the full function of the mind and its rich potential.

However, there is one more instance I would like to cite, first because of its unusual character and secondly because it links us into our consideration of communication.

Ronnie Davis was six when he came to me and had no speech. Besides, he fluctuated in behavior from passive withdrawal to the violent activity of a small tornado. And he was not toilet trained.

He had passed through a number of medical and psychiatric diagnostic programs — his grandfather was an oral surgeon — but the conclusions varied to such a degree that nothing could be gained from them, except from the reported interviews with the parents and grandparents. Ronnie lived with his grandparents.

His mother was not yet married when she found herself pregnant with the child and had tried to rid herself of the burden. After the birth she became very ill and could not care for the child, so her parents took him. On her recovery she returned to her husband's cattle ranch without the baby because, she said, the house was so small they had to build on another room for him before she could have his necessary paraphernalia around. During her illness she had developed a noticeable stammer.

The only person with whom Ronnie showed any inclination to relate was the grandfather. Every evening he would crawl into the

Cindy's first self-likeness, established by correlating the body circles with triangle and square shapes.

Cindy's representation in oil of a friend's head, an example of visualization extended successfully into the rich mental province of the imagination.

grandfather's lap, curl up like an embryo in the womb, and go to sleep.

At our first meeting, in my home, I knew this child had to get himself born. I had not the least idea how, but it *had to happen*.

I arranged a small table with a lighted candle in the middle and we sat across from each other. If nothing else, the fascination of the flame would hold his attention for awhile. I watched his bright blue eyes. One eye fastened on the flame, then the other took over. I blew softly causing the flame to bend toward him.

He drew back and looked at me quickly, fearfully. But he looked with *both* eyes. And *our gaze held.* I scarcely breathed; then, at last, I smiled at him and he relaxed, glancing at the flame again and back to my eyes. *He had come out!*

From there, you can guess the phases we went through from birth to six, teaching the vehicles, opening the channels, establishing acceptable patterns. Control came, speech came, interests and relationships came as each growth in function fell into place.

This was the only child I ever had who learned to make the written symbols for speech sounds by observing and visualizing the candle flame as the breath, during speech, played upon it.

One day, while we were playing with clay in the garden, a tiny beetle crawled onto Ronnie's hand. He held up his hand and examined the little creature with great care. Then he giggled. "Can you hear him?" he asked.

"Is he making a noise?"

"Yes, he's talking to me." His face glowed.

"Can you understand him?"

"Well, almost. He's got an awful little voice."

"You'll have to sharpen your ears and learn his language," I told him. "Maybe, we could find out his name and where he lives and what he eats . . ."

Thus a study of bugs began. We read books and wrote stories — about bugs as we studied them and also what Ronnie said the bugs told him and what other animals told him about bugs — and amassed a creditable insect collection, and made no gesture toward curbing or disproving the far flight of his imagination. (Maybe, he *did* hear the bugs talking!)

At any rate, he is a young man now, in college, taking pre-med and hoping to specialize in the diseases carried by insects. His communication has come into focus on the wave-length of all mankind.

7. Learning is Communicating

COMMUNICATION, it has apparently been determined, comes into effect while the child is still in the womb. After birth, it follows him through the whole of his living. Like education, indexed as self-development, communication starts at the beginning and continues to the very end. Unlike education, however, which centers within the human unit, communication spreads out from that which takes place within, radiates into every facet of life, wherever voice or influence reaches, and often far beyond that.

Obviously, we can only touch on a few points in this inclusive and most comprehensive subject, points which directly apply to the NH Child. By understanding where the progression in communication might have broken down, we are sometimes able to help a child that has baffled other types of inquiry into his difficulty.

To be successful communication must be a happy, reciprocal giving and receiving between two or more transmitters, audibly or inaudibly broadcasting. Should the inaudible transmitting between a mother and her child — nine months in the womb and probably the greater part of childhood — prove successful, it provides the base on which the complex structure of human fulfilment rests. Further it is necessary that all inaudible sending and receiving — the dialogue that goes on within the human unit, the impressions and expressions that pass in and out through the senses, and the desires, conclusions and plans in the mind — be successful, loved and wanted to insure the profit of that which comes after.

What comes after? Speech. Writing. Reading. In that order.

Where a block appears in speech, inquire first into and mend the preceding areas of communication. Often there is nothing else to mend, and speech comes naturally.

Maria Montessori has said: "A child who is happy will speak. A child who draws will write. When a child knows how to write he will read."

One development follows hand-in-hand upon the other in natural ordered sequence. Our modern school requirements are top-heavy, over emphasizing *Reading* without first building a supporting foundation underneath. Build the foundation and reading comes, almost without effort, just for fun.

Tommy's visualized reproduction of fruit forms done in infantile style. One development follows the other in a natural, ordered sequence.

Tommy's representation in oil of a horse and cat.

How is this achieved? After cooperation has been established and relaxation has taken effect to the point where the child can sit still and listen I begin reading stories to him. Even if he is unable to talk yet, we act out the stories — letting grunts and gestures take the place of spoken words — and draw pictures about them. These are evidence of comprehension of the story content and practice in recognizing story structure. All the while that the sense vehicles are being trained these reading activities go on, often with stories that utilize the sense effectively on which we are working. Frequently, we write our own story, the child creating, I writing. And it is such fun to act these out or make their illustrations.

Then we enter the influence of concentration. All children I have, young ones, old ones, those with speech and those without, are given the experience of learning the written symbols for speech sounds from the formation of the mouth and the use of the breath during periods of concentration. Even those who already know how to write well are fascinated with it. It is a new approach, a new knowledge for them. When the letters are learned, the child then writes his stories by himself. I spell the words for him — we do not take the effort for spelling until much later — and he writes.

Let no one be misled. These stories children write are no "I see Dick — I see Jane" type. How adult writers determine that such content is right for child perusal has always been a mystery to me. They should see some stories written by children that have real life situations and action, as well as live child vocabulary. Their stories are charming.

While we are enjoying these new and very exciting adventures, I keep on reading to the child from books. Now, however, I give him a copy of the book, too. He turns the pages with me and learns how to start at the top of the left hand page, following along line by line with his finger as I read. Thus he sees how to begin at the left of each line and progress across the page to the right, then flash quickly to the left hand of the line below. When that page is finished, he understands, by experience, how to go quickly to the top of the right hand page and start the process over again from left to right, line by line. This pattern confuses many children.

All at once, as we come to a word he has used in his stories several times, I will stop reading and let him call the word, which he does eagerly, glowing with pride.

Soon, we are reading aloud together, synchronizing our phrasing and inflections so his ear and his thinking become tuned to meaningful expression from the cold type. This can be done with small groups as well as individually. At this point of progress, I can stop anywhere and the child — or children — is or are able to recognize and call the needed word, even say the complete sentence, then a paragraph.

Yet, while he is now communicating happily with written symbols in word sequence, he is not reading. That complicated mental process comes only when he finds an absorbing interest into which he can plunge with his whole heart and soul. To illustrate, I would like to tell about little Teanie Tuttle coming to the place where he actually learned to read.

At three Teanie's difficulties were so pronounced that his father and grandfather, both M.D.s, began a widespread inquiry into the prospects of help for him. They lived in St. Louis, Missouri, and after exhausting local possibilities turned to the east and the west.

Each diagnostic and training center added another descriptive term to Teanie's type of deviation from the standardized norm. The compiled list covered everything from severely mentally retarded to schizophrenic. And each center stated that it was unable to treat his difficulty. Then, just before he turned four, he was brought to my door.

I remember thinking as I first looked at him, "He is an angel taken flesh." His particular gold and pink beauty struck me, inside. And as long as I had him I was always aware of this angelic quality about him.

This first day, he broke from his mother's hand, ran past me, like a dancer on his tip-toes, to a plant growing in the hall and began patting and muttering to the leaves. His hands moved like butterfly wings fluttering on a leaf where the creature was about to suck the honey. I made note: when we reach for a point of interest it will be with growing things.

It took over two years for us to balance the score between Teanie's deviations and himself. Even then, the balance had an odd aloof character. Teanie seemed unable to unbend and be an ordinary human child. He was very dear and pleasant, and very cooperative, but there was no positive drive for or against anything. He ran into my arms each morning in delight at seeing me and in anticipation of the day, but there was no real affection in the gesture. His speech, which had been language in reverse, was now clear but sparse and colorless. The stories he wrote were short and dry, and he read with me because I invited him, not because he found fun in it.

All along the way we had planted things, observed the seeds crack, the plant and root unfold, the whole structure flower and seed, to be planted again. And only when the leaves came out was

Randy's In-Depth, done in collage, illustrates communication between the child and himself.

he truly engaged in the operation. Then he petted and loved the leaves, and sometimes wrote stories about them.

On our third spring together we planted a vegetable and flower garden outside. And one day when we were working in the garden the neighbor's cat came strolling over to see what we were about. Teanie had always been frightened of animals, so I began stroking the cat to show him how friendly the creature was. The cat rolled over on the ground to have his under-neck and stomach rubbed and I finally persuaded Teanie to stroke him.

Stroking, and finding the fur soft and pleasant, he pressed more firmly with his hand over the cat's breast, and felt its heart beat.

Teanie jumped as if the startling discovery gave him a shock. "That's the cat's heart," I told him. "The cat has a heart that beats just like ours does. Feel your heart?" I put his hand over his own heart.

The amazed wonder in him seemed to fling open some closed doors inside, and I stood there looking through them, seeing this child communicate with himself for the first time.

Suddenly he put one hand back on the cat's heart, the other he kept over his own. His listening attitude was mature and professional. At last he said, "His heart is different."

"How?" I asked.

"Different. Just different."

"All right, come inside. We'll look in a book about hearts and find out how a cat's heart is different."

So Teanie's consuming interest arose from an entirely unsuspected source. Thereon, the gap in communication between the child and himself — his self image — between himself and his not-self — the world he contacts, physically and mentally — and between his orbit and that of the energy called life was bridged in one momentous leap.

8. The Vital Parental Dimension

Parenthood, wise men say, is the most
fulfilling and the most rewarding of human experiences, as well as the
most perplexing and exacting. Added to this, the parents of the neurologically impaired have that singular opportunity for personal growth
and understanding service presented only to those able to accept a great
challenge.

For this reason, when taking a child with whom I intend to work, I
always turn to the parents for their invaluable assistance in launching the
course we must follow. They are not merely supporters of the program
for their child, they are active participants and vital cooperators in the
entire effort. I need their respect and concern for the child, the dynamic
vigor resident in their hopes and expectations for his ultimate accomplish-
ment. Without the vital participation of the parents the effort is watered
down to a simple effort, passably effective, no matter how much stoic
determination is exerted, and often never quite reaching the goal.

The recognition, and the application, of the parental dimension in the
effective educating of the child is the *fourth basic principle* on which
educative success rests.

Parents live with the child from birth to adulthood. Who has more
at stake in his yield than they? Who else would turn his life inside out
for the child if that is the need? Who stands by, more than any other,
through all vicissitudes, watching, encouraging, providing, teaching, hoping, praying? It seems to me that it is our job as *temporary* guides for
the child to liberate this great potential in his favor, to liberate it from
anxiety and self-condemnation, from despair and frustration and put it
to work in consequential ways.

There is a magnifying of collective potencies in this triangle —
mother-father-teacher. Possibly by showing how this sort of a team works
some of its puissance may communicate:

> The first time I asked a parent to help me with a child was early
> in my attempts at befriending these children with baffling problems.
> Mrs. Sullivan brought her son Dick, age eight, to my house in a
> frenzy of despair. The boy had not yet developed speech and now
> he had begun sitting in a corner with his face to the wall most of
> the day, sucking his thumb.
>
> "Can't you *do* something?" she begged.

Because, at that time, I did not know what to do, and no one else seemed to know what to do, and because my heart bled for the frustrated woman, I replied, "Maybe, if you and your husband would help me, we might try to work something out."

"Help *you?*" she cried, and began to weep.

The family, she related haltingly, was in imminent danger of disintegrating into its separate units — the boy to an institution, the mother and father to their individual ways. Each parent accused the other of some gross misdemeanor that had caused feeble-mindedness in their off-spring, and the tension had grown more than either of them could bear.

"Look," I said, "if you had intended to give up without, at least, one more try, you wouldn't have come to me. And I'm willing to try *with* you. You can't tell what we might come up with."

The first try surprised and inspired us. Together we planned and took a trip to a nearby trout farm. There, with the help of all three adults, Dick caught a trout. As he pulled it out of the water, his father's hands taking the weight, he let out a scream of delight that could have been heard in the next state.

Then, while he handled the wriggling creature, I urged him to say its name, using the crest of his delight as a lever. At last, he made a fair production of the word.

His father gasped, "Did he say . . . *fish?*"

"He tried," I told him. "With another try, he'll do it."

Mr. Sullivan grabbed the boy and hugged him. "Son," he said, "we'll build a fish pond in the back yard and you can catch a fish every day!" And they did, together.

During this term of companionship Dick stopped sucking his thumb and added twenty words to his vocabulary besides *fish.* Also during this term of communication Mr. Sullivan discovered that his son adored him. If the boy had enough sense to love, to talk and learn how to make a pond and catch fish, what could stop him from learning everything?

Aside from building the pond the boy and his father spent an hour each evening playing games that developed eye-hand coordination and making camping equipment for trips into the mountains. Mrs. Sullivan gave an hour each morning with Dick learning to relax together, to sing and practice the word building which I assigned Dick each day after school hours.

On the weekend we three — father-mother-teacher — put our heads together and "brain-stormed" the next move. As Dick acquired skill enough in listening, thinking and speaking he joined the planning period. Only in participation in family planning is a child able to learn how to prepare for wise action and evaluate mistakes and shortcomings in the true light of learning.

In one of these conferences we took up the prospects of Dick going to school. He was now nine, growing huskier and more confident every day. It was time for him to find himself in the world of his peers. We frankly discussed the fact that the only place to begin this venture, to insure some control of the situation and be able to count on some success from the start, was at the bottom of the pile — in the Kindergarten. A few months' trial there and he could matriculate to the next level. I had inquired into such an arrangement with a cooperative school district outside the town where we lived.

It took the combined persuasiveness of his father, his mother and me to get Dick to consent to this procedure. His father finally added an ample reward, and he agreed.

The morning we arrived at the school I left him on the play ground while I went into the office to check the arrangements. I was to return in a few minutes and go into his room with him. As I came back onto the play yard I saw Dick surrounded by a crowd of jeering five-year-olds: "What's this big giant doing in our yard? Get out, big kid!"

Dick was as white as a sheet, his eyes glazed with terror. I held out my hand to him and he showed no sign of recognition. We walked into the classroom with the others and sat down at a vacant table. He still did not seem to know me, or know where he was. I did not confuse him further by trying to explain.

When the teacher gave instruction about getting clay from a jar in the corner, I urged him up and went with him. Automatically, he scooped out some clay with his hands, turned and handed it to me. Memory was returning. Then he took some for himself and we went back to the table. As he grasped the clay in both hands to make a ball — as we had done together many times — he looked across the table at me and smiled. He was himself.

"Are you all right?" I asked. He nodded. "Then we must go up and meet your teacher. She is very nice. You will like her."

Two months later Dick was ready to go into an experimental First Grade where reading was delayed until the child was fully prepared by an enriched readiness program. Our family discussion on that move was conducted at a different level of relationships. Dick pivoted the conference.

Bringing up his problem of getting along with the other boys, his father contributed, "When I went to a new school . . ." His illustration showed how he had met the same difficulties, overcome some of them and lived with his own blunders when he failed to solve some.

Apprehensive about his teacher liking him, his mother contributed, "I found out that my teachers . . ." She offered suggestions of being helpful in the class so the teacher might find it possible to praise him for good citizenship, setting the pattern for all around acceptance.

Dick's whole being glowed. At last he belonged. He was sharing that intimate world which a close-knit family knows and in which he had been a stranger before. Now, the three of them — father-mother-son — made that cogent triangle. From here on, my role was a minor one, watching over Dick's progress year by year.

There are, of course, a few parents who are hard to persuade that this relationship is necessary or that it is any concern of theirs. Such was Dr. Blandon, an electrical engineer on an important government project, and his handsome wife.

The only way I was able to explain the fact that the whole family came to the initial interview, concerned with obtaining help for the boy Terry, age ten, was on the grounds of their insatiable curiosity. They all came to see what kind of a person I was and if I had any idea of what I was talking about. And all of them were handsome to look at: two boys, fourteen and seventeen, Terry, and little Betty, six.

Dr. Blandon started the conversation with a detailed account of Terry's high intellectual rating and his high development in all the areas not requiring academic achievement. Besides this, he had speech and behavior problems, neither of which, Dr. Blandon pointed out, were important.

"Everyone has made too much of his problems," he concluded. "He likes the attention."

"But poor Terry doesn't get any attention," Mrs. Blandon complained. "You and the boys . . ."

Here a verbal sparring bout ensued, each taking a nicely aimed poke at the other. Terry sat looking from one to the other, like a spectator at a tennis match. It ended with the two older boys triumphantly making the final statements, and proving, without doubt, who got the attention.

"Is this the kind of discourse to which you were referring, Mrs. Blandon?" I asked. She nodded. I turned to the head of the family. "And what do you do at home when your two sons take over like this, Dr. Blandon?"

"What can you do?" He spread his hands. "Some experts say to take a strong hand, others say to keep hands off. None of them seem to have the answer, really."

"Suppose all of us sat down and pooled our ideas of what is right to do just for your family, no one else. We might come up with something everyone could agree to that would make your discussions enlightening and helpful."

"Now, look," Dr. Blandon cut in quickly, "we're not throwing the whole family in your lap. We only came to bargain for Terry."

"Terry is an integral part of the family. I can't bargain *for* him without bargaining *with* the rest of you."

"Well, yes, but you see," he demurred, "we're a pretty independent bunch. We have encouraged independence in our children, and we let each other alone, to give or take on his own. It's the same on the job. When I'm given a project to do, I don't ask the whole crew to help me. I know what to do, and I do it on my own."

"What happens when you hit a snag?"

Dr. Blandon looked at me, then down at his hands. "Well . . . you've got me there . . ."

"You, as a family, have hit a snag in Terry. Something has gone wrong. I'll be glad to act as a consultant whom you have called in, if you want me to. But you're the crew on the job, all of you. And you know more about the situation and about Terry than anyone else. I can merely add a fresh breath into an atmosphere which seems to have gone stale. When your thinking clears you will come up with the answers. Do you want to get on with it, or not?"

"Let's get on with it," Mrs. Blandon said.

Billy Vale also had a father engaged in a high-level government project. He was a biochemist. Billy's mother was Iranian, carefully educated and well-traveled, and deeply religious — an affirmation not shared by her husband.

Billy was ten and the oldest child in the family, with a younger brother and sister. The entire family had superior capacity and everyone except Billy put it to good use. He could not retain knowledge, reason logically or devise creatively. Therefore, he had arrived nowhere in school.

Not a single member of the family hesitated in accepting the opportunity of helping Billy in his particular embarrassment. It appeared as if they had been sincerely searching for such a chance, wanting to absolve, no doubt, their troubled concern for him.

For fun, at Billy's first visit, we took to fingerpaints. He verbalized with every stroke of his hands: "I'm a dumb-ox, you know that? I'm stupid, like . . . a . . . a gillie. That's what the kids call me . . . Gillie-Billie. Everybody's smart but me . . . my whole family's smart . . . they think I'm an idiot . . . they don't say so . . . but they think it . . . I can tell. When I don't throw a ball straight . . . they look at one another . . . I can tell. When everybody's reading and I'm not . . . I can feel them thinking it . . . Oh, he's an idiot . . . say, I'm sure making a mess out of this .. . . ."

On and on he went, deprecating himself for nearly the hour, messing up one attempt at a picture after another. The last one, he happened to let the corner of the paper slip down over the rest of it as he put it on the floor to dry. When he picked off the offending corner it had made an interesting design. There was a little elf, as plain as day, sitting under a large leaf beside a pond.

When the family came to pick Billy up and saw the fingerpaints, they exclaimed enthusiastically, almost in a single voice, "Oh, how I'd like to do something like that! Couldn't we do some?"

"Are you all nuts?" Billy cried. "This is kid's stuff, Dad!"

"Do you know, Bill," his father replied, "I've been so busy all my life I've never had time to do anything arty. Who cares if it's kid stuff? I can't wait to get my hands in that paint!"

"I can't either," his wife agreed.

So Billy and I fixed aprons and papers and places on tables to suit each size and showed all of them how to fingerpaint. Billy taught his mother and father, and I helped the children.

Looking at the results, Billy became excited. He could see figures and flowers and trees in the swirls and festoons of paint, in fact he had a wonderful faculty for seeing these misty, half-formed beauties. The family rose to the occasion. "Where . . . where do you see that, Billy?" one would cry. "Show me, Billy," another would urge. "Right here . . . and over there. Right over there! Can't you see that, stupid?" Billy was rising to the occasion, too.

"Billy, you have the best eyes in the family," his mother praised. And his father harmonized, "He certainly has! I would never have seen that temple in my picture if you hadn't pointed it out, Bill. And it's as plain as the nose on my face."

Such delicious approval could not be allowed to wane. So Billy suggested that they take paint and paper home and have another painting session that evening. Which they did.

This came to be a nightly exercise for some weeks. Through practice and a new bent for experimentation, Billy's pictures proved interesting enough to be put into frames and get on the walls of their home — which was something, because they had an elegantly appointed home. Finally, some of their friends wanted his pictures and a few of Dr. Vale's associates on the government project became enamored with the fingerpaints, hanging them in their offices. Billy was now a celebrity.

This tremendous boost to his morale vitalized his very core and set every cell in him to functioning. With the minimum of training in various avenues of need, he was soon reading and writing and calculating arithmetically. Now reading at home on art and art values became a whole family engagement. Friends who liked to discuss art were invited in and Billy, in his turn, was allowed to express his opinions, listened to respectfully.

Then, one day, he executed a design in lacquer that he named LISTENING IN DEPTH. The only suggestion of form in it might be of clouds swept by the wind, but the colors and the implication of expanding depth carried a remarkable impact.

In our weekly conference, a few days later, Billy explained how he had felt while working on the design and what he saw in it. "I felt as if I were inside the breathing part of me," he said. "The white ran into the yellow and it seemed that I was that color, breathing, shining all over . . . but in the middle . . . right here . . . I wanted to see a spot of blue . . . like you say Dad . . . a symbol of myself . . . in myself. And something seemed to say to me . . . 'God looks into your pure self and sees Himself . . .' "

His mother sat gazing at him, her mouth open a bit in silent amazement. At last she said softly, "Billy . . . you have found the words. I could never find the words . . ." She turned to look at her husband.

He was staring at the floor. Perhaps caught in his own inner listening.

9. Crossing the Bridge to Public School

THE FINAL PRINCIPLE on which we who educate stand when helping the NH Child realize his fullest possibilities is a bridge between his very special way of learning and public school expectancy into which he must eventually matriculate. Of all the crucial periods in the child's life so far, this is one of the most critical. Everything that has been accomplished up to this point can be undone by wrong attitudes and practices.

To this bridge construction we must bend every effort, as well as every creative idea for its design that we can muster. School administrators and teachers need help in understanding the crucial character of this bridging, in understanding the delicate balance of the child at this juncture, his persistent resistances and his continued claim on individual considerations.

Most NH Children refuse to be told *what* to do and *how* to do it without first accepting the proposed action or activity on their own terms, relaxing with it and finding reason and profit in the doing, seen in the light of their own special interests. They hold this attitude in common with all our new children, but hold it more rigidly. This must be recognized and the attitude directed into meaningful and beneficial efforts during the bridging step, and, in some cases, accounted for in the program past it.

I recall a little girl, Jeannie Whittle, who entered public school after three years of learning in a special way. She had achieved in all school subjects to about a Third Grade level, above that in reading, but considering her age and her need for adjustment the school administrator placed her in a regular Second Grade. (At that time there was no awareness of the need for bridging from where she was to what she must be for regular classroom procedures.)

Jeannie was given a seat in the back of the room, the farthest distance she could be from the sight of her teacher's face and sound of her teacher's voice. Naturally she heard and saw nothing that was explained or demonstrated.

She was given a Reading Workbook that, she was told, would show whether she understood the stories in the reader that accompanied the Workbook. The reader was an old one to her. She had read all the stories in it, had dramatized most of them, both acting in and directing them, and had written stories of her own based on the story structure of those in the book. So there was no question of her comprehension, but she refused to do the work in the Workbook. She said the directions in it were silly and asked nothing of interest to her, so she would not do them.

For continued, determined refusal, she was retained two and a half years in the Second Grade, in spite of all attempts to bring about an understanding between the school and the child. At last, frustrated, rejected and ridiculed, she developed psychotic behavior and had to be taken out of school.

Now a number of classes to serve this purpose of bridging are being formed, or are already in operation. Most of those in operation seem to be merely watered down versions of regular classroom procedures. The results in such situations can be tragic. It is to the yet unorganized classes, and to those being re-organized, that we earnestly address the following:

1. Through the initial four weeks of the class carry on the same learning structure on which the student prospered beforehand —

(a) The teacher meets each student individually and orients him into the new environment before the whole class meets.

(b) Small class, below ten, if possible.

(c) Firmly established routine maintained.

(d) Democratic government within established structure . . . student planning and law enforcement.

(e) Each student competes only with himself.

(f) Relaxation and concentration practiced.

(g) Periodic self-evaluation (group counseling) to maintain positive attitudes.

(h) Student's choice of interest allowed full freedom, within group concession.

(i) Teacher's guidance by discussion and suggestion and inspiration.

(j) Student kept at highest peak of performance by self-imposed pressure (inspired by teacher).

(k) Creative writing and dramatics maintained as major tools.

2. Added specifications in the class design — which probably were not required in the previous situation —

(a) A large enough room, or rooms, where, besides study tables or desks and individual foot-lockers, building, planting, arts and crafts, experimental projects, dancing and staging of plays can be easily accommodated. There should also be library and thinking corners, and individual sanctuaries marked with students' names.

(b) A tutor for special help, planned for all students, that none be singled out. Private help should be carried out in the individual sanctuaries, not in another section of the school building.

(c) A special subjects teacher should not be introduced the first week, and the first month or so special subjects should be given in the classroom, not in the special subjects' rooms.

(d) Rules and know-how for playground activities must be taught to the children in these special classes, they can not acquire them vicariously as most children do, then kept closely supervised for a time when allowed to participate on the playground so their play relationships will be successful.

3. After the fourth or fifth week gradually undertake the necessary changes in class routine and teaching procedures —

(a) Discuss and illustrate each step in the change with the students, showing reasons and profits, and gain their acceptance before advancing.

(b) Demonstrate the differences between educative and instructional processes in simple short lessons where the students participate.

(c) Repeat this at intervals, until the student is able to understand and operate under the new process and method.

(d) Keep a program balance for some time between instructional and educative procedures. State each time which process is being used.

(e) Review often from the beginning of the introduction into the new method.

(f) Keep the program balanced during the whole year with creative and sifting-searching-analytical activities. Thus, the NH Child can thrive.

(g) Let each student judge his own progress . . . without the use of report cards, if at all possible.

The bridging process can never be accomplished unless there is complete understanding and cooperation between the home and the school. The hours and methods of homework, the amount and type of pressure, inspiration or encouragement needed, and the setting and re-setting of goals for the child must be thought through and agreed upon by teacher and parents, together. The importance of the vitalizing vigor in this co-ordinated action can not be over emphasized. Too long home and school, in separate camps, have carried individualistic ideas and policies concerning the child's progressive development, each camp defensive of his boundaries and of what he thinks of as his job. Now, with the NH, there *must* be unity or progress turns in reverse. This forward step should then lead into unified action for all agencies concerned with children.

Thereby, the successful posturing of the child's life as it flows smoothly over the bridge from where he is to where he is intended to go, also sets in motion a greater flow toward a larger goal, toward a realized fullness in living. Education — self-unfoldment — was purposed to this end.

10. The Beauty of Diversity

REFERRING to the effect of meaningful experiences, a learned man once said, "Now, the commonplace is shot through with new glory, old burdens seem light, and a crown is placed above our heads that for the rest of our lives we are trying to grow tall enough to wear."

So we stand tall, at last, and see the commonplace shot through with glory. Problems that once seemed too dire to face now become light; in the glow of the crown over our heads old failures turn into fresh opportunities.

Who among us can now look at a neurologically impaired child without seeing a beautiful human being with rare potential who is in great need? And who would now spare himself until that child's need is met? So it is that the *first principle* — our attitude about a brain-damaged child — has begun to operate effectively.

The next principle — changing the child's attitude about himself — then appears possible after the first step is taken, even while it takes more thought and effort to set it in motion. However, once set in motion, the acquisition of the art of cooperation, relaxation and the coordination of well-trained senses — the process by which the child comes to know and respect himself — never stops working for him through all the years of his life. Nor can the cardinal effects of this principle be ignored in the total educational picture for all children.

The third step toward our goal unlocks the potential — ". . . the imprisoned splendor" — and gentles it for use. Merely to open the gates and let the creative energy run wild in useless dissipation is unpardonable, as it is unpardonable to expect the wisdom and maturity from a child sufficient to organize and transform *instructionally* implanted material to his mental growth. Carefully and gently the released energies are *led out,* guided into meaningful channels through *concentration,* organized by *visualization* and brought into productivity by the creative use of the *imagination.* The result: a profitably educated child who can one day become a profitable world citizen.

Mounting to the fourth principle where the parents are recognized as the dominant unit sustaining the child far into the future, we pause in appreciation of the part they play. The importance and the weight of this unit in the success of the whole program is probably beyond measure. And we must help it to function wisely. Its tremendous leverage in the child's life is ignored to his detriment, but its power, brought into service, works miracles — peculiar miracles that change so-called abnormalities to singular virtues. This has been proven many times over.

The last principle is a bridge over which the neurologically handicapped child walks into the normally prescribed activities and classroom procedures. The leap from this child's special learning area into that which is commonly considered suitable for the average child is too difficult and too fertile with the possibility of failure to take without a bridge. This transitional period for the NH Child must incorporate the procedures with which he is familiar to establish confidence, then a gradual and carefully planned introduction of the general classroom expectancies can be fruitfully accepted. Though such a program is expensive and unwieldy for the public schools it pays off in the long run. Perhaps, present legislation enacted to cover the added expense of the NH Child's education could be extended to private schools offering this bridging service. However managed, the imperative obligation to provide such a transitional interim can not be evaded.

In a final retake: the education of the neurologically impaired stands on five basic principles — 1. the attitude of the educator (parent or teacher); 2. the attitude of the child; 3. the educative process employed as an exercise of self-development and communication at all levels: 4. the recognition of the parents' vital measure in the entire process; 5. the provision of a successful period of transition for the child between special consideration for his needs and his absorption into the main stream of living. At each step, for each child, the methods and techniques for achieving these goals are necessarily created for a particular need at a particular moment. Though the techniques so created can be tried with another child, as a primer, they seldom show effective results. If parents and teachers have the courage to work creatively, it has been proven, all the right ways and means reveal themselves, as though by some fundamental law that balances a need.

Observing these creative processes take hold and reshape lives there is an impression, very strong and real, of standing tall. From this position we can look far. Every reshaped life, like a charged drop of water in the ocean, changes the future intent of things as the reshaped life impregnates life around it with new energies and fresh impulses drawn from the failures and victories through which it passed. To me, the face of the future appears clear. Look with me:

1. Note the great numbers of children being born with neurological impairment. Veritable legions. Considering the type of potential most of them possess, can we, in all reasonableness, continue to speak of them as an accident, a mistake of nature, a burden and a bane? Rather, shouldn't we look for possible estimable rea-

sons for their tremendous influx? Could they be regarded as a vanguard in human evolution introducing to modern man the inescapable condition by which and because of which he must learn to use the vast unopened areas of his brain? Man would never move out of experienced, time-rutted pathways unless forced to it.

Arthur's result of pressing one finger painting over another. The freedom found in creative development — and the joy it brings — will infiltrate all education.

What wonderful new creative thinking men might be doing in the future with fresh brain areas to use!

2. On the same level with this latter prescient view is the eventual issue from the present rash of experimental studies and research projects concerned with the structure and the function of the brain because of the urgent need to diagnose brain-injuries more accurately and determine the prognosis. Having confirmation now at hand that the brain is not the seat of intelligence, merely the instrument acted upon by impulses from another source, is it likely, as it

seems reasonable to suppose, that research will continue until the nature, the extent and actual residence of intelligence is found?

When the brain-damaged, himself, joins in this search with his fresh point-of-view, no doubt a new frame of reference will arise. Could it also be called a new frame of *reverence?*

3. Further far looking shows signs of teacher and pupil coming closer together, searching, discovering and learning side by side. Teachers who have once let go of old concepts of teaching while working with NH Children could never return to that rigid formula, any more than a chick could return to his shell. So the freedom they find in creative development and the joy it brings will infiltrate all educational centers. Its ease and effectiveness, once experienced, will sell creative education to all those coming in contact with young people.

4. Future schools appear, at the end of a long lane of change, to be evolving into educational *centers,* quite different than the present set standard of classroom, building and learning schedules. The centers, located in areas where young people will be able to *experience* what is written about in books, and experiment creatively on their own, will require few buildings and large land areas. It is entirely possible that parents, now looking forward to greater leisure time, will join their children in these new age thinking and production colonies. Self-unfoldment should never cease.

5. Tomorrow's family unit is also clearly delineated in the present. At the turn of each new year the family unit becomes less cohesive as a pyramid of authority and more cooperative as a contributing cell in community life. More often than not, both parents work and the children at a very early age become self-sufficient in their home and community, oriented for control and direction. This conditions children to emotional detachment from the father-mother image to mental allegiance to community leaders and community values whereby they gain acceptance and personal satisfaction in living. Will this satisfaction lead progressively to the recognition and acceptance of the community called *mankind* as the leader and director of human effort?

So we move toward ever broader horizons — mutating and creating as we go, unfolding anew out of the broken parts of the old. Thus "old injuries become *light* . . .", revealing DIVERSITY, not conformity, in the basic stones on which the glorious WHOLENESS of the future is built.

THE END